Teaching with Rhythm and Rhyme

In honor of
my first teacher, my mother,
Irene Reid Morris

and to

my first grandchild,
Katelyn Rose Caughman

Teaching with Rhythm and Rhyme

Resources and Activities for Preschoolers Through Grade Two

by
GINGER MORRIS CAUGHMAN

McFarland & Company, Inc., Publishers
Jefferson, North Carolina, and London

ALSO BY GINGER MORRIS CAUGHMAN

Church Library Promotion: A Handbook of How-Tos
(McFarland, 1990)

Library of Congress Cataloguing-in-Publication Data

Caughman, Ginger Morris, 1939–
    Teaching with rhythm and rhyme : resources and activities
for preschoolers through grade two / by Ginger Morris Caughman.
      p.   cm.
    Includes bibliographical references and index.
    ISBN 0-7864-0811-1 (softcover : 50# alkaline paper) ∞
    1. Early childhood education — Activity programs.   I. Title.
LB1139.35.A37 C39   2000
372.13 — dc21   00-32871

British Library cataloguing data are available

Cover art © 2000 Eye Wire

Manufactured in the United States of America

McFarland & Company, Inc., Publishers
  Box 611, Jefferson, North Carolina 28640
    www.mcfarlandpub.com

Contents

Acknowledgments

In appreciation to:

- My husband Bill for his love, encouragement, and practical help — thank you, dear!
- My children Cathy, Bill III, and Sharon for their loving support;
- Carol O'Regan, my friend, for her beautiful artwork;
- My family and friends for support and prayers;
- My pastor Bro. Joe Molchanoff and my church family;
- Bill III, Sharon and Mike for help with my new computer;
- The St. Charles Parish Library — Mary des Bordes, director, and all the staff, especially the reference questions to Julie, Phyllis, Dianna, Yvonne, and Shawn;
- My son, William Luther Caughman III, for excellent legal advice;
- These for special assistance with permissions and copyright: Linda Wallace, John Y. Cole, Liz Durkin, Debi Lindaberry, Carol Christiansen, Virginia Copelin, Muriel Blackwell, Margaret Barker, Ivey P. Wallace, Salima McTaggart, Andrew Au, Cynthia Stilley, Joan Boyes, Hank Ketcham, Dottie Robertson, and Suzanne Morovic;
- All my teachers in Kentwood, Louisiana;
- My teachers in these universities: MSCW and UNO; and
- My principals and co-workers on the faculty in Columbus and Natchez, Mississippi; and New Orleans, Norco, and Des Allemands, Louisiana,

I sincerely thank you all.

–gmc

Introduction

Rhythm and rhyme are a part of a happy childhood.

Rhythm is measured motion, a flow, a movement. Our hearts beat in a regular rhythm. We breathe in a natural rhythm. Words, speech, and language have a flow, a rhythm. Patterns in timing, spacing, accents, and repetition all produce rhythm. Poems, music and singing have rhythm. In music regular recurring elements of groups of strong and weak beats alternate to produce rhythm. Children have an intrinsic sense of rhythm and enjoy the sounds and patterns of words, poems, stories, music and songs.

Rhyme is the regular repetition of a sound especially at the end of lines in a poem or a word.[1] Children are delighted with the singsong repetition of rhyming letters, words, poems, and stories. Boys and girls like to repeat rhyming words, sing with rhymes, and participate in activities utilizing rhymes. These include clapping hands, bouncing balls and jumping rope. Young children enjoy hearing and learning to say the traditional "contagious rhythms"[2] of Mother Goose and nursery rhymes.

Young children have a short attention span. Physically they can't sit still very long.[3] Use rhythm and rhyme activities to provide variety and needed movement for developing minds and bodies.

Teaching young children with both rhythm and rhyme is the focus of this work, which is intended as a resource for teachers and librarians. Those who have chosen to be a teacher have chosen a difficult but worthy profession. In the words of a master teacher, a teacher needs "a clear head and a warm heart."[4]

Young children love their teachers. I remember each of my elementary school teachers at Maude Arnette Grammar School and could recite their names in a jump-rope rhythm for you: Grade 1, Mrs. Daisy Key; Grade 2, Mrs. Elva Covington; Grade 3, Mrs. Juanita Lambert; Grades 4 and 6, Miss Ethel Joyal; Grade 5, Miss Mary Lucille Napier; Grade 7, Mrs. Frances Bell; and Grade 8, Mrs. Helen Singleton. I appreciate each of my many teachers. Especially am I grateful for the excellence of Karen Harris, Juanita Lambert, Maude Cheek, Emma Shepek, Maude Walker, Mary Frances Mitchell, Dolores Baker, and Elizabeth Bowne Minn.

"Mother" at home is everyone's first teacher. My worn copies of *Mother Goose* rhymes and *A Child's Garden of Verses* from which my mother read are among my treasured possessions. I read these poems with joy and satisfaction to my own children and in schools to my student-children.

Writing has expanded my joy of teaching to include you, the reader of this book. Teaching via writing is both exciting and humbling. I hope you will find practical help, encouragement, and enjoyment in this volume. I am grateful to the many involved in the process of the production of this book.

This book is for classroom teachers and librarians in public and private schools; teachers in nursery schools and kindergartens; child development centers, and day care; librarians for public library storytime; parents in home schools; babysitters; parents and other relatives and friends playing with children at home. The book will be a practical college text for classes in "Early Childhood Education" as well as a valuable resource for all Elementary Education majors. Enjoy teaching with rhythm and rhyme. Enrich your teaching by utilizing the information herein.

Teaching with Rhythm and Rhyme provides Mother Goose rhymes, nursery rhymes, finger plays, and poems for you to read or recite. Music is printed for songs and games. Stories about the childhood of some great musicians are included, out of interest in the rhythm of their lives. The rhythm of color and the seasons are explored, all-important for the young child. The beauty and rhythm of sign language is introduced. Seasonal school year activities are included for the cyclic rhythm of the beginning, ending, then starting again of a school year.

Appendices include snacks and recipes as well as a list of resources and addresses.

Teach with rhyme and rhythm,
Teach with rhythm and rhyme,
Teach with music,
And teach with song,
Teach with rhythm and rhyme!
— Ginger M. Caughman
Norco, Louisiana
Spring 2000

1

Mother Goose Rhymes

"NO, NO my Melodies will never die,
While nurses sing, or babies cry."
                    — Mother Goose

Who was Mother Goose? Not the author of the rhymes, but only the name for a collection of anonymous verses told and retold before seeing print. The rhymes came from England and the name from France.[5] The dictionary even has an entry, actually two listings, for Mother Goose: "1. The imaginary narrator of a collection of tales (1697) by Charles Perrault. 2. The imaginary creator of a collection of nursery rhymes first published in London in 1765."[6]

In French, Mother Goose is "Ma Mère l'Oye." Charles Perrault's book used the name "Mother Goose" but the collection had only eight fairy tales and no rhymes. Some of the fairy tales are still popular today such as "Little Red Riding Hood," "Cinderella," and "Sleeping Beauty."[7]

The term "Mother Goose" is a part of our cultural literacy. Many use the name, including Hollywood. In a male version of the famous goose, Cary Grant assumes a role of "Father Goose" in the title movie. In the plot, Grant had a following of people to care for, much like "The Old Woman in the Shoe" who had so many children she didn't know quite what to do.

Some have criticized the nursery rhymes as being violent or too filled with English politics. But many of the rhymes have stood the test of time. Don't deny children the opportunity to hear, repeat, sing and play with Mother Goose and nursery rhymes. Parents, grandparents, aunts and uncles are continuing to repeat these rhymes to babies and young children. One thing that has made the rhymes so endearing to generations is the repetition of the rhythm and the expected rhyme. Teachers are many times the source for those who have never heard the rhymes. They should try the ones included in this chapter and scattered throughout this book. Choose your own favorites. Relax and have fun with the rhythm of the rhymes.

Numerous editions of Mother Goose rhymes have been printed. Go to your library or favorite bookstore and look at some old and new editions to choose your favorites. Let children see many editions. Read and let their imaginations create illustrations.

One year in a school library I dressed as Mother Goose. What fun. Some younger children thought I really was Mother Goose. And so I was for a day.[8] You can be "Mother Goose" or "Father Goose." Read or recite a rhyme to your children today. Mother Goose rhymes truly belong to everyone!

Old Mother Goose

Old Mother Goose, when
She wanted to wander,
Would ride through the air
On a very fine gander.

Mother Goose had a house,
Built deep in a wood,
An owl at the door
As a watchman stood.

She had a son Jack,
A plain-looking lad,

He was not very good,
Nor yet very bad.

She sent him to market,
A live goose he bought:
"Here! Mother," says he,
"It will not go for nought."

Jack's goose and her gander
Grew very fond;
They'd both eat together,
Or swim in the pond.
Jack found one morning,
As I have been told,
His goose had laid for him
An egg of pure gold!

Jack rode to his mother,
The news for to tell
She called him a good boy,
And said it was well.

And Old Mother Goose
The goose saddled soon,
And mounting its back,
Flew up to the moon.

Mother Goose (photo by the author; doll by Rosemary Donaldson; quilt by Helen Singleton).

Cloudy Weather

One misty, moisty morning,
When cloudy was the weather,
I chanced to meet an old man clothed
    all in leather.
He began to compliment, and I began
    to grin,
How do you do? How do you do?
How do you do again?

Pussy Cat

I like little pussy, her coat is so warm,
And if I don't hurt her she'll do me no
    harm;
So I'll not pull her tail, nor drive her
    away,
But pussy and I very gently will play.

Bo-Peep

Little Bo-peep has lost her sheep
And can't tell where to find them;
Leave them alone, and they'll come
    home,
Wagging their tails behind them.

Nanny

Little Nanny Etticoat
In a white petticoat,

And a red nose;
The longer she stands
The shorter she grows.

Jack

Jack, be nimble;
Jack, be quick;
Jack, jump over
   the candlestick.

"Jack and the Candlestick" by Joey Weber.

The Moon

I see the moon,
The moon sees me;
God bless the moon,
And God bless me.

"The Moon and Space" by Alexis Delauneville.

Play for Babies

How many days
Has my baby to play?
Saturday, Sunday, Monday,
Tuesday, Wednesday, Thursday, Friday,
Saturday, Sunday, Monday.

Pat-a-Cake

Pat-a-cake,
Pat-a-cake,
Baker's man.
Bake me a cake
As fast as you can.
Pat it and prick it,
And mark it with a B,
And put it in the oven
For BABY and me.

"A Cake for Baby" by author.

Hickety, Pickety

Hickety, pickety, my black hen,
She lays eggs for gentlemen.
Gentlemen come every day
To see what my black hen does lay.

The A B C's

A, B, C, D, E, F, G,
H, I, J, K, L, M, N, O, P,
Q, R, S, and T, U, V,
W, X, and Y and Z.
Now I've said my A, B, C,
Tell me what you think of me.

Jumping Joan

Here am I,
Little jumping Joan,
When nobody's with me
I'm always alone.

Little Miss Muffet

Little Miss Muffet
Sat on a tuffet,

"Miss Muffet on Her Tuffet" by Carol O'Regan.

Eating some curds and whey;
Along came a spider,
And sat down beside her,
And frightened Miss Muffet away.

Lady with Music

Ride a cockhorse
To Banbury Cross
To see a fine lady
Upon a white horse.
Rings on her fingers
Bells on her toes
She shall have music
Wherever she goes!

Mary Morey

I'll tell you a story
About Mary Morey,
And now my story's begun.
I'll tell you another
About her brother,
And now my story's done!

Hot Cross Buns

Hot cross buns! Hot cross buns!
One-a-penny, two-a-penny. Hot cross
    buns!

Hickory Dickory Dock!

Hickory dickory dock!
The mouse ran up the clock.
The clock struck "one,"
The mouse ran down!
Hickory, dickory dock.

St. Ives

As I was going to St. Ives
I met a man who had seven wives.
Every wife had seven sacks,
Every sack had seven cats.
Every cat had seven kits.
Kits, cats, sacks and wives,
How many were going to St. Ives?

Humpty Dumpty

Humpty Dumpty sat on a wall,
Humpty Dumpty had a great fall;
All the king's horses and all the king's
    men
Couldn't put Humpty Dumpty
    together again.

Star Light

Star light, star bright,
First star I see tonight.
I wish I may,
I wish I might,
Have the wish
I wish tonight.

The Mulberry Bush

Here we go round the mulberry bush,
The mulberry bush, the mulberry bush,
Here we go round the mulberry bush,
So early in the morning.

Pease Porridge Hot

Pease porridge hot,
Pease porridge cold,

Pease porridge in the pot,
Nine days old.
Some like it hot,
Some like it cold,
Some like it in the pot,
Nine days old.

To Market

To market,
To market,
To buy a fat pig.
Home again,
Home again,
Jiggety, jig.

"A Fat Pig" by Carol O'Regan.

Mistress Mary

Mistress Mary,
Quite contrary,
How does your
    garden grow?

With silver bells
And cockle shells
And pretty maids
All in a row.

"Flowers" by Carol O'Regan.

London Bridge

London Bridge is falling down,
Falling down, falling down,

London Bridge is falling down,
My fair lady.

Build it up with iron bars,
Iron bars, iron bars,
Build it up with iron bars,
My fair lady.

The Muffin Man

Oh, do you know the muffin man?
The muffin man? The muffin man?
Oh do you know the muffin man
Who lives in Drury Lane?
Oh yes, I know the muffin man
The muffin man. The muffin man.
Oh yes, I know the muffin man
Who lives in Drury Lane.

Bye Baby Bunting

Bye baby bunting.
Daddy's gone a-hunting,
To get a little rabbit skin
To wrap the baby bunting in.

Mother May I?

Mother, may I go out to swim?
Yes, my darling daughter:
Hang your clothes on a hickory limb
But don't go near the water.

A Man of Words

A man of words and not of deeds
Is like a garden full of weeds.

For the Want of a Nail

For the want of a nail, the shoe was lost,
For the want of a shoe, the horse was
    lost,
For the want of a horse, the rider was
    lost,
For the want of a rider, the battle was
    lost,
For the want of a battle, the kingdom
    was lost,
And all for the want of a horseshoe nail!

Old King Cole

Old King Cole
Was a merry old soul,
And a merry old soul was he
He called for his pipe,
And he called for his bowl,
And he called for his fiddlers three.

Cock a Doodle Doo

Cock a doodle doo!
My dame has lost her shoe,
My master's lost his fiddle stick,
And knows not what to do.

Rain, Rain

Rain, rain, go away,
Come again another day
Little Johnny wants to play.

Hey Diddle Diddle

Hey diddle diddle, the cat and the
    fiddle,

The cow jumped over the moon.
The little dog laughed to see such
    sport,
And the dish ran away with the spoon.

One Flew East

One flew east,
One flew west,
One flew over
The cuckoo's nest.

Pussy Cat

Pussy cat, pussy cat,
Where have you
    been?
I've been to London
To visit the Queen.
Pussy cat, pussy cat,
What did you there?
I frightened a little
    mouse
Under the chair.

"A Little Mouse" by Joey Weber.

This Little Pig

This little pig went to market,
This little pig stayed home,

"This Little Pig" by Carol O'Regan.

This little pig had roast beef,
This little pig had none,
And this little pig cried,
"Wee-wee-wee,"
All the way home.

Daffy-Down-Dilly

Daffy-down-dilly
Is now come to town
With a petticoat green
And a bright yellow gown.

This Mother Goose rhyme is a riddle. For the answer see Chapter 2, page 21.

Peter Piper

Peter Piper picked a peck of pickled
    peppers;
A peck of pickled peppers Peter Piper
    picked.
If Peter Piper picked a peck of pickled
    peppers,
How many peppers did Peter Piper
    pick?

Answer: One peck. "Peter Piper picked a peck of pickled peppers."
This old nursery rhyme is a tongue twister and children enjoy trying to say all of the words. There will always be many variations of rhymes and tales that have been in the oral tradition for many years. I learned this "Riddle and Tongue Twister" the way I've written above. Another variation changes the last line: "Where's the peck of pickled peppers Peter Piper picked?" Instead of the question, "Where?" I prefer "How many...?"

The Grand Old Duke of York

The grand old Duke of York,
He had ten thousand men;
He marched them up to the top of the
    hill,
And marched them down again.

And when you're up, you're up.
And when you're down, you're down.
But when you're only half-way up,
You're neither up nor down!

I found several versions including: the *Brave* Old Duke of York; the *Royal* Duke of York; and the *Grand* Old Duke of York. My preference is the third version which I heard and played as a child. You may choose to substitute "brave" or "royal" for "grand." See motions for the game on page 23.

Baa! Baa! Black Sheep

Baa! Baa! Black sheep,
Have you any wool?

Yes, sir, yes, sir!
Three bags full.

One for my master
And one for my dame,

And one for the little boy
That lives in the lane.

Baa! Baa! Black sheep,
Have you any wool?

Yes, sir, yes, sir!
Three bags full.

Questions: In the nursery rhyme, how much wool did the sheep have? How are the bags of wool used? How is wool sheared? Get the story of wool and see photos of spring and summer wool-shearing in Massachusetts. Read *Spring Fleece: A Day of Sheepshearing*. The text and black-and-white photographs are by Catherine Paladino.

Mary Had a Little Lamb

Mary had a little lamb
Its fleece was white as snow.
And everywhere that Mary went
The lamb was sure to go.

Lamb followed her to school one day
It was against the rule.
It made the children laugh and play
To see a lamb at school.

And so the teacher turned it out,
But still Lamb lingered near,
And waited patiently about
'Till Mary did appear.

"Why does Lamb love Mary so?"
The eager children cried.
"Why, Mary loves Lamb, you know!"
The teacher did reply.

Mary was real and the events of the nursery rhyme actually happened in New England in the 1800s.[9] Mary was Mary Elizabeth Sawyer (1806–1889) of Sterling, Massachusetts."[10]

"Mary Had a Little Lamb" is in the old "Volland Popular Edition" given to me in childhood. Mary and her lamb are with many more Mother Goose melodies listed in the back without illustration.[11]

Bartlett's credits John Roulstone (1805–1822) as author of the first three stanzas and Sarah Josepha Hale (1788–1879) for completing the poem to six stanzas. A story about the poem (1928) by Mr. and Mrs. Henry Ford gives these sources plus declaring the events in the narrative as true.[12]

The poem I heard at home was a bit different from the one we sang and learned in grade school. I've reproduced the poem for you as I remember it from the oral storytelling tradition. Learn the music on page 62 in Chapter 5 and sing with your class. Children will enjoy the charming illustrations by Tomie de Paola in his book *Mary Had a Little Lamb*.[13]

Little Boys and Little Girls

What are little boys made of, made of?
What are little boys made of?
Snakes and snails and puppy dog tails;
That's what little boys are made of,
     made of.

And what are little girls, made of, made of?
What are little girls made of?
Sugar and spice and all that's nice;
That's what little girls are made of,
     made of.

Ring-Around-the-Roses (3 Versions)

1) Ring-around-the-roses
A pocket full of posies;
Upstairs, downstairs,
We all fall down.*

2) Ring-around-the-rosie,
A pocket full of posies;
One, two, three,
And we all fall down!*

The Flint Public Library Preschool Storytellers use the following version[14]:

3) Ring around the rocket ship
Try to grab a star.
Stardust, stardust
Fall where you are.*

(*Motions:* All join hands and circle to right. At word "grab," drop hands and reach up.)

*On the last line, all the children fall down. The last one to fall leaves the game.

Numerals

One, two. Buckle my shoe.
Three, four. Shut the door.
Five, six. Pick up sticks.
Seven, eight. Lay them straight.
Nine, ten. A big fat hen!

For numbers to use with this nursery rhyme, use a pencil to lightly trace the numbers you need. Cut numerals from a sturdy poster board and laminate. Or for an interesting tactile experience make the numbers from sandpaper. Note: Turn the 6 over for a 9! Use the numbers in many other ways in your classroom. See page 43.

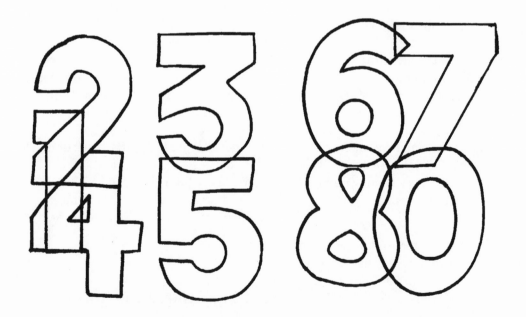

"Numerals 1 to 10" by author.

2

Activities with Mother Goose Rhymes

Mother Goose Activities

1. **Travel by Flying Carpet.** Have each child bring a small throw rug to sit on. Take the children on a "Magic Carpet Ride" during Mother Goose emphasis or at other times during the school year. Use the magic carpet idea for

- Reading Mother Goose rhymes
- Reading fairy tales
- Letting the children watch or participate in acting out rhymes or stories
- Letting a child sit before the class, "pretend," and tell an original story to the class. Note: Did you ever hear the radio show *Let's Pretend*?[15]

2. **Mother Goose Rhymes.** Read, recite, repeat, sing, and act out Mother Goose rhymes. Watch children's faces. Involve them in the activities. Suggestions can be found throughout the book.

3. **Mother Goose Stories.** Mother Goose was the name of Perrault's French *Tales of Mother Goose* (1697). They were not rhymes at all but stories we call fairy tales or folk tales[16]: "Cinderella," "Little Red Riding Hood," "Puss in Boots," "Tom Thumb," and others. Read folk tales and fairy tales to the children. Let them act out stories with or without props. Almost any of the fairy tales are good material for drama. Try these:

- "The Three Billy Goats Gruff"
- "Henny Penny"
- "The Gingerbread Man"
- "The Three Little Pigs"
- "The Three Bears"

- "Little Red Riding Hood"
- "The Little Red Hen"

4. **Mother Goose Class Book.** Let each child make a picture of a favorite Mother Goose character. Let the class decide on a title. Make a cover and a title page. Put pictures together in the "book." Write on the title page:

- Book Title. Name children have decided upon.
- Write: "Illustrated by Children in [Name teacher or grade] Class."

5. **Individual Books.** Make individual books of nursery and Mother Goose rhymes. Let child illustrate.

6. **Class ABC Book.** Make a class "ABC Book." Assign each child a letter. Ask them to bring a picture from a magazine or draw a picture of their letter. Put together in a class book. Be sure to include a title page.

7. **Book Character Day.** Have a school-wide Mother Goose Character Day. Let various classes dramatize favorite books or stories at a school-wide gathering in the auditorium, cafetorium, school library, or on the playground.

8. **Book Friends.** Ask each class in school to make a booklet of Book Friends. Have them include a cover and title page. Display booklets in the school library.

9. **Celebrity Readers.** Invite celebrities to come to your school and read books to the children. Invite school administrators, the public library director, parents, grandparents, aunts and

Previous page: *"Little Miss Muffet" by Carol O'Regan.*

uncles, library trustees, local government officials, sports and movie stars, television and radio personalities, and local authors. Write and call early as these are all busy people. When you issue the invitation ask if they have a favorite book from childhood they would like to read to the children. Have books ready to suggest in case your "stars" don't bring a favorite of their own. Ask your librarian for help.

10. **Mother Goose Bookmark Contest.** Plan a bookmark contest for first and second graders. Give out rules. Enlist judges. Have a winner at each grade level. Reproduce the winners' drawings in bookmarks for the entire school.

11. **Mother Goose Day for Parents and Grandparents.** Encourage reading at home! For your situation you might prefer a "Night of Reading" or a night devoted to emphasizing reading: reading at home; the teaching of reading at school; the recreational reading in the school and public library.

- Invite guest speakers.
- Have stories, read books or give book talks.
- Serve light refreshments.

12. **Choose a character** and develop a theme for:

- a day
- a week
- a year!

You can develop themes for many classroom or school-wide activities by choosing one Mother Goose character and developing an emphasis for a day, a week, or a year! Example: See "Humpty Dumpty" Activities on pages 16–17. This idea will be particularly useful for:

- Kindergartens
- Schools devoted to pre-kindergarten through Grade 2
- Child day-care centers
- Parents who home school

Note: Be sure your theme is not an end in itself[17] but is a vehicle to help you achieve your curriculum goals. The exception would be when your purpose is *fun.* Remember in planning anything to consider your time, energy, and purpose. But then enjoyment can be part of a purpose, can't it!

Characters You Could Develop Into a Theme

A short list of characters is provided that you can develop into a theme. Suggestions are also given for planning occasions for their use. This will start you thinking. Brainstorm with other faculty members of your grade level. Or let the ideas play in your mind as you do chores at home tonight. Read through the rhymes yourself and find others. Look earlier in this chapter; read your personal childhood book, or check out Mother Goose rhymes from the library. Develop lessons, themes, or promotion from these and other characters:

- "Jack and Jill" — A boy and a girl character to use in teaching manners or review discipline rules. Or put a book in their pail for reading emphasis. Decorate the wall of a reading center.

- "Peter, Pumpkin" and "Mistress Mary"—Spring, Nature, growing themes.
- "Mary and Lamb"—August or September; beginning school.
- "Little Boy Blue with His Horn"—Music class; learning a song. Place a nametag of trumpeter Wynton

"Horn sticker."

Marsalis on the boy dressed in blue with a golden horn.

- "Jack Be Nimble" and "Jumping Joan"—Fitness emphasis. Use with physical or mental exercise. Make pictures of Jack and Joan jumping. Explain meaning of the word "nimble."[18]
- Does "Little Miss Muffet" know E. B. White's Charlotte?[19]
- The "Old Woman's Shoe" enlarged holding a photograph of each child in your class.
- Have "Wee Willie Winkle" hold up a lantern. (See title page of this book.)
- Let all children wear crowns (see page 130) and be either the "Queen of Hearts" or "Old King Cole."
- "Queen of Hearts"—Valentine's Party.

Humpty Dumpty Activities

1. **On the Wall**. Draw Humpty Dumpty sitting on a brick wall. Add color with paints or felt tip markers. Use captions: ON THE WALL (all capitals). Humpty Dumpty (upper and lower case lettering).

2. **On the Wall Bulletin Board**. Make a bulletin board with Humpty Dumpty sitting on the top of a brick wall. Cover the bulletin board with light blue art paper. Buy brick paper to cover a little more than half of the bulletin board. Use captions as shown in #1.

3. **On the Wall. Large Bulletin Board.** Decorate the board as shown in

#2. Surround Humpty Dumpty with the children's artwork or writing.

4. **Individual Character Box**. Let each child make a Humpty Dumpty box or let them choose another Mother Goose character to prepare for their character box.

- Have each child bring a shoe box from home. Have a few extras on hand.
- Ask teachers and parents to save the plastic egg stocking containers.
- Begin collecting shoe boxes and plastic eggs several weeks before your art project.

- Let each child cover an individual shoe box with paper or paint. Cover the box and top separately so the top will be removable. Let glue or paint dry.

- Decorate the egg to look like "Humpty Dumpty." Draw with permanent markers on the plastic sur-face. Or glue bits of material, yarn, or buttons to make face, hair, and clothes.

"Humpty Dumpty" by author.

- Mount the plastic egg on top of the shoebox "wall."

- Label the box. Let child choose their caption. For preschoolers you might want to glue on prepared printed labels. For beginning read-ers and writers let them letter a simple phrase such as: "Humpty Dumpty" or "On the Wall" or something funny like "Wall Fall."

- Use box as a container for the week's writing, artwork, book-marks, or buttons to take home on Friday.

5. **Display:** "On the Wall." Prepare one shoe box as directed in the individ-ual boxes in #4. Choose one of these dis-play places:

- Place "Character Box" on library check-out desk during an emphasis of "Mother Goose Rhymes."

- Place on the top of the library shelf where the "Mother Goose" books are located. Call attention to the location during a library lesson.

- Place in the school office during Children's Book Week.

- Use in classroom on teacher's desk; on a shelf under a window; in a book nook or reading area.

6. Give out **prepared bookmarks** with illustrations of Humpty Dumpty or other Mother Goose characters. See ordering information on page 160.

7. Sponsor a **schoolwide bookmark contest** during a Mother Goose Week, November Children's Book Week, or another time best for your school calen-dar. Suggest a theme. Have a separate contest for each grade.

8. Have a **classroom bookmark contest**.

Dress-Up Book Characters

A resource list of Mother Goose book characters is below. Use it to help children decide how to dress for Dress Up Day! Read parts of the list to them until they decide one they'd like to dress-up to represent. Children may find other characters in the rhymes. I found these in my childhood Mother Goose.

"My Mother Goose" by Carol O'Regan.

Resource List of Mother Goose characters

- Peter, Pumpkin Eater and Peter's Wife
- Polly with a Teakettle and Sukey
- Lady-bird
- Old Man in Leather
- Little Bo-Beep, Shepherdess
- Nanny Etticoat with Red Nose, Wearing a White Petticoat
- Jack and Jill with a Pail
- Nimble Jack
- Crooked Man with Cat
- Mary with Lamb
- Tommy Tittlemouse, Fisherman

- Willie Boy with Rake (To Hayfield)
- Wee Willie Winkle, in Nightgown
- Old Woman in Shoe with Switches
- Old Woman and Calf
- Little Tom Tinker and Dog
- Jumping Joan
- Simple Simon, En Route to the Fair
- Maid with No Nose, Holding Blackbird
- Johnny Stout and Johnny Green
- Tommy on Stick Horse, Riding to Banbury Cross
- Little Miss Muffet on Tuffet with Spider; Muffet is Holding a Bowl, Spoon
- Three Wise Men of Gotham
- Polly Flinders, Sitting in the Cinders
- Thief Tom with Pig
- Tardy Schoolboy and Teacher
- Tommy's Nurse, Pat a Cake
- Sleepy Little Boy Blue with a Horn
- Lucy Locket, and Kitty Fisher, Pocket with a Ribbon
- Tom Tucker
- John, One Stocking On, One Off
- Humpty Dumpty on a Wall
- Old Mother Hubbard
- Jack Horner, Plum on Thumb
- Queen of Hearts with Tray of Tarts and Knave of Hearts
- Margery Daw, on a Seesaw

- Daffy-Down-Dilly; Wear a Green and Yellow Gown

- Old King Cole and Three Fiddlers, with Pipe and Bowl

- Mistress Mary, Gardener

"Student bookmark contest."

Planning a Children's Book Week

1. Get teachers together who are especially interested in reading. Let them plan an appropriate emphasis for the needs of your school.

2. Decide on the dates for your emphasis. If the third week of November isn't convenient for your school, choose other dates. Choose tentative dates, clear dates with adminsitration, then set dates, and inform the faculty. The entire school should look forward to the week.

3. Enlist others to help, depending on the elaborateness of your plans. Enlist faculty, children, parents, and the community as appropriate.

4. Make specific plans. Suggestions follow.

5. Plan promotion. Publicize school-wide. Notify parents. Take pictures for the community newspaper.

6. Evaluate after any major emphasis to help plans for the next time.

7. Read these suggestions, brainstorm ideas, and choose activities appropriate for your children.

- Daily read children's books!

- Have a Book-Character Dress-Up Day. Enlist judges. Give prizes for costumes in various categories. Give *something* to every child (such as a bookmark, button, sign, or a sticker).

- Follow the National Children's Book Week theme or choose a theme. Order promotion materials related to your theme.[20]

- Celebrate Reading!

- Celebrate Books!

- Enjoy Children's Books!

- Encourage children to visit public libraries weekly with their family.

- "**Travel by Flying Carpet.**" Have each child bring a small throw rug to sit on during this emphasis.

- **Mother Goose.** Read, recite, repeat, sing, and act out Mother Goose rhymes. See Chapter 1 for more suggestions.

- **Folk Tales.** Read folk tales and fairy tales. Act out stories with or without props. Use "The Three Billy Goats Gruff," "Henny Penny," "The Three Little Pigs," "The Three Bears," or other favorites.

- **Make Books.** Let each child make a picture of a favorite book character. Let class decide on a title. Make a cover and a title page. Put pictures together in a "book."

- **Class Book.** Make a class book of nursery and Mother Goose rhymes.

- **Books.** Make individual books.

- **Book Character Day.** Have a school-wide Book Character Day. Let classes dramatize favorite books or stories. School-wide attendance in auditorium, cafetorium, school library, or playground.

- **Book Friends.** Ask each class to make a booklet of **Book Friends.** Include a cover and title page. Display all booklets together in the school library.

- **Celebrity Readers.** Invite celebrities to come to your school and read books to the children. Write and call early as these are all busy people. When you issue the invitation ask if they have a favorite book from childhood they would like to read. Book suggestions: *The Very Hungry Caterpillar*, Eric Carle; *Goodnight Moon*, Margaret Wise Brown; *The Little Engine That Could*, Watty Piper; *The Story About Ping*, Marjorie Flack; *The Little House*, Virginia Burton; *Millions of Cats*, Wanda Gag.

- **Bookmark Contest.** For first and second graders plan a bookmark contest. Give out rules. Enlist judges. Have a winner at each grade level. Reproduce the winners drawings in bookmarks for the entire school. (Winners from some of my school bookmark contests are reproduced on pages 19 and 53.)

Bake Hot Cross Buns

Hot cross buns!
Hot cross buns!
One-a-penny,
Two-a-penny.
Hot cross buns!

     — Mother Goose rhyme

Suggestions:

- Let the children make "Mother Goose Hot Cross Buns."

- Enlist an aide or parent helper to take buns to the kitchen to bake.

- Make prior arrangements with the kitchen staff to use their oven.

- Enjoy hot buns in class.

Ingredients:

1 package of ready-to-bake dinner rolls or biscuit dough
½ cup raisins
½ teaspoon cinnamon
1 Tablespoon of sugar (or use cinnamon-sugar)
Glaze: Use 1 egg and 2 Tablespoons heavy cream
A can or tube of icing

Directions:

1. Separate rolls and place on an ungreased baking pan. 2. Stick a few raisins in the top of each roll. 3. Brush the glaze on the top of each roll. 4. Sprinkle sugar and cinnamon over the top of rolls. 5. Bake the rolls according to package directions. About 10 minutes at 375 degrees. Longer for biscuits. Cook until brown. 6. Squeeze icing in a cross on the top of each roll.

Activities:

- Make in the Spring or at Easter time.

- Bake any time of the school year.

- Count to ten. Use to help motivate all children to be able to count to ten. Get a roll of new pennies from the bank. Have each child count out ten pennies before eating one of the hot cross buns!

Riddles in Mother Goose

Read or recite these three riddles from Chapter 1. Let children guess riddle.

1) "As I was going to St. Ives..."
See page 7 for rhyme.
Question: How many were going?
Answer: ONE!

2) "Little Nannie Etticoat"
See pages 5–6 for rhyme.
Question: How can this be?
Answer: Nannie is a CANDLE!

3) "Daffy-Down Dilly"

See page 10 for rhyme.
Question: Who is "Daffy-Down-Dilly?
Answer: She is a flower: the daffodil!

"A White Candle" by Joey Weber.

Mother Goose Rhymes

Recite the Mother Goose rhyme "Little Boys and Little Girls" to a class. Just for fun divide the class into two groups, boys and girls. Have the children line up in two rows facing each other. Play with the rhyme of the Mother

Goose jingle. Children enjoy the internal rhyme of snails, tails and spice, nice.

Variations: To vary the above, try one of these four suggestions:

1) Have the boys recite the first stanza and girls the second.

2) Have the boys begin the rhythm asking the question in the first two lines. Let girls respond by answering what boys are made of. Vice versa with the second stanza about girls. Let girls ask question in first two lines and boys answer with the last two lines.

3) Proceed as in #1 or #2 with this addition. At the end of the rhyme, add one line, letting children say in unison: "That's what we are made of, made of."

4) Choose one from #1–#3. Then add a line letting boys say, "... boys are made of," and let girls say, "... girls are made of." See Change #4:

Little Boys and Little Girls

What are little boys made of, made of?
What are little boys made of?
Snakes and snails and puppy dog tails;
That's what little boys are made of,
    made of.

And what are little girls made of, made of?
What are little girls made of?
Sugar and spice and all that's nice;
That's what little girls are made of,
    made of.

(Conclusion in Unison. Boys and Girls Speak at the Same Time!)
(Boys:) That's what little boys are made of, made of.
(Girls:) That's what little girls are made of, made of.

Add Motions

Motions and drama can be added to many of the Mother Goose and nursery rhymes. Read these from Chapter 1 and let children add actions:

MOTHER GOOSE RHYME	MOTIONS
• This little pig went to market.	Touch and count fingers or toes.
• One, two, buckle my shoe.	Count and arrange ten sticks.
• Humpty Dumpty.	Stand and fall.
• Peas porridge hot.	Partners clap each others hands.
• One misty moisty am.	Class chooses partners acts out.
• Jack be nimble.	Read, recite, then jump.
• Pat a cake.	Rub hands together. Draw letters.
• Ring around the roses.	Form circle. Stand up, down, then fall.

See Chapter 1: This little pig, pages 9–10; One two, page 12; Humpty dumpty, page 7; Peas porridge, pages 7–8; One misty moisty, page 5; Jack be nimble, page 6; Pat-a-cake, page 6; Ring-around-the, pages 11–12.

Drop the Handkerchief

All of the children except one who is "it" form a circle facing in. "It" is given a handkerchief, scarf, or old rag and begins skipping around the outside of the circle. The children chant the rhyme in a sing-song manner. "A tisket, a tasket, a green and yellow basket…" When the group reaches the words "I dropped it," the handkerchief is dropped behind a child in the circle. That child quickly grabs the handkerchief and runs after the first player. When the first player is caught and tagged (touched) with the handkerchief, the first player is a captive in the middle of the circle and the second player is "It." Play continues in like fashion until children tire of the game.

Drop the Handkerchief

A-tisket, a-tasket,
A green and yellow basket.
I wrote a letter to my love
And on the way I dropped* it.
I dropped it! I dropped it! I dropped! …

*Some versions say "lost" for "dropped." I played and learned the rhyme, "I dropped it!"

Game: The Grand Old Duke, Two Versions:

1. **Outside Game:** "The Grand Old Duke" Game #1.
Purposes: Fun for children. A very active version of the game gives a physical outlet for the children's energy.

Directions:

- Choose one child as the Grand Old Duke.

- All children line up by "The Duke" but facing a designated boundary (such as a fence or tree or another teacher) which is the TOP OF THE HILL!

- The Duke with arm and hand raised gives a ONE WORD DIRECTION (Such as: march, run, skip, gallop) and then drops hand signaling, "GO!"

- The children dash off to the top of the hill and back. The first one to arrive back to beginning point is the "NEW DUKE."

- Repeat game until children tire of it, everyone has a turn, or recess is over.

2. **Inside Game:** "The Grand Old Duke": Game #2:
Purposes: Enjoyable game for children.
Note: This version can be played in a small space as we did in Mrs. Lambert's 3rd Grade on rainy days when I was a child. Happy memories. Directions:

- Children repeat rhyme marching in place. See rhyme, page 10.

- Walk forward two or three paces.

- Then walk backward two or three steps.

- The FUN and challenge is the second verse. Stand tall at the word "up"; stoop down at the word "down"; then try to hold a position in the middle without moving. The first one to move has to sit down and is out of the game. Continue playing until one player remains. All applaud (clap) for the winner who becomes the Grand Old Duke.

Optional: You may want to reward the winner with a paper crown to wear the rest of the day. For directions in making a paper crown, see pages 130–132.

Singing Game and Dance

"Oats, Peas, Beans and Barley Grow"

[1st Verse Directions: One child, the farmer, stands in the middle of a circle. The children dance around the farmer singing verse one. (Music, page 67.)]

1. Oats, peas, beans and barley grow;
   Oats, peas, beans and barley grow.
   Do you, or I, or anyone know
   How oats, peas, beans and barley
   grow?

2. Thus the farmer sows his seed,
   Then he stands and takes his ease;
   He stamps his foot and claps his hands,
   And turns around to view his lands.

3. Waiting for a partner,
   Waiting for a partner,
   Open the ring and choose one in
   While all the others dance and sing.

4. Tra, la, la, la, la, la, la,
   [Repeat tra, la, la in rhythm to end.]

Directions:

2nd Verse: Children imitate actions in words: sowing seed; standing straight with arms folded; stamping foot and clapping hands; and turning around to look at the fields.

3rd Verse: The children circle around singing. At the words "open the ring and choose one in" the farmer chooses a partner. The children break the ring to let the farmer's partner join him in the center. The circle closes back up and all dance and sing.

4th Verse: The circle stands still. All children clap and sing. The two in the center dance around. The child chosen is the new farmer and the game repeats.

The Mulberry Bush

1. Here we go round the mulberry bush,
   The mulberry bush, the mulberry
   bush,
   Here we go round the mulberry bush,
   So early in the morning.

2. This is the way we wash our clothes,
   Wash our clothes, wash our clothes,
   This is the way we wash our clothes,
   So early in the morning.

3. This is the way we iron our clothes…

4. …

Notes:

- Add as many other verses as you desire. Or let the children think of motions to add as they sing.

Here We Go Round

This version of "The Mulberry Bush" has words and actions for each day of the week:

1. Here we go round the mulberry bush,
   The mulberry bush, the mulberry bush; Here we go round the mulberry bush, So early in the morning.

2. This is the way we go to church...
   (etc.)
   So early SUNDAY morning.

3. This is the way we wash our clothes...
   (etc.)
   So early MONDAY morning.

4. This is the way we iron our clothes...
   (etc.)
   So early TUESDAY morning.

5. This is the way we mend our clothes...
   (etc.)
   So early WEDNESDAY morning.

6. This is the way we sweep the house...
   (etc.)
   So early THURSDAY morning.

7. This is the way we scrub the floor...
   (etc.)
   So early FRIDAY morning.

8. This is the way we make the bread...
   (etc.)
   So early SATURDAY morning.

Directions (See music in Chapter 5, page 68.)

1st Verse: The game begins as the children join hands, form a circle, sing the first verse and dance around to the left: walking, skipping, or gliding.

2nd Verse: Drop hands and turn to face inside the circle. In the last line of each verse the children reutnr to the circle formation and repeat the first verse as a chorus.

3rd and other verses: The actions are suggested by the words.

Happily Introduce Children to Mother Goose at School and Home!

Child development centers and day care teachers often have babies through age five when children enter pre-school, nursery, and kindergarten programs in public and private school. Many parents across our land are now home-schooling their children. As teachers you can also point out to parents the values of speaking and reading word rhythms, Mother Goose rhymes, nursery rhymes, poems and stories to their child. Use these facts for parent conferences or faculty-parent meetings:

Say the lyrical Mother Goose rhymes casually at home or school during the day. Besides an introduction to English poetry children enter kindergarten and first grade: with better speech habits; a more creative use of words; a greater feeling for words; "expanded imaginations; increased vocabulary; and a developed ear for the music of words."[21]

Use Mother Goose Rhythms for a Speech Exercise

The main reason for using Mother Goose rhymes is for enjoyment! But May Arbuthnot suggests two unusual and helpful uses of Mother Goose rhymes and rhythms:

1. Speech teachers, classroom teachers, and parents. Use Mother Goose rhymes as the "best possible speech exercise." Have children repeat the rhymes for fun (*not as a drill!*) and "the improvement in speech agility is surprising."[22]

2. Foreign-born children who do not know English. Children can learn English rapdily from hearing and saying Mother Goose rhymes which will help them "catch our characteristic speech rhythms in the process."[23]

3

Move with Rhyme and Rhythm

Young children are extremely active, with short attention spans. They have a physical need to move. Plan activities and lessons that allow them to change positions often and meet this developmental need. This chapter suggests many activities combining movement with rhythm. Mother Goose and other nursery rhymes from the previous chapter can be repeated in rhythm, dance, story, and other enjoyable activities. The chapters of the book overlap and are filled with other suggestions for play. Many of these activities can be used either inside or outside.

Follow the Leader

Select one responsible child to be first. Have the children form a line behind the first child. Instruct the children to follow the leader and initiate whatever the first person does. Be available to make suggestions if needed and to supervise any potentially dangerous actions.

This old game is tried and true. Children delight to play "Follow the Leader." Some children will think of creative activities to imitate. You may need to help others think of activities. Perhaps you will be the first leader. Hop, sing, wave hands, skip, run, clap hands while walking. Or make suggestions from some of the activities in the next group.

Moving Activities with Nursery Rhymes

- Gallop while reciting "Ride a cock horse." See rhyme on page 7.

- Walk normally while repeating "To market, to market." See page 8.

- March while quoting "Marching, marching, here we come" (Robert L. Stevenson), page 100.

- March to the cadence of "The Grand Old Duke of York." Pause at the words "up" and "down" and "stand tall" or "stoop down" as the words indicate. See page 10.

- Skip to the lines of "Lou, Lou, skip to my Lou."

- Hop like a rabbit. Say, "Hop, hop, hop, hop;" then suddenly one command to "stop."

- Dance and move to the "Alphabet Song" letting children try to form the letters with their hands, arms, and bodies.

- Pretend to be autumn leaves. Dance and sing to the song "Autumn Leaves Are Falling." See page 73.

- Move like bells in the lovely song "Lovely Evening." See page 72.

- Move and play the singing games.

Previous page: *"Fun with Balloons" by Carol O'Regan.*

Moving Activities with Nursery Rhymes

- Sing and play "The Mulberry Bush." Choose from three versions depending on the children's ages. One is in Chapter 5: Music, page 68. Two versions are on pages 24 and 25.

- A children's favorite from many generations: "The Farmer in the Dell." See page 64.

- Play "London Bridge." See page 8 for the rhyme.

- Run outside in a line hollering "Oooh-ooh-ooh-ooh-ooh" like little Indian braves and squaws. Move hand on and off the lips, changing the sound. Then let the line of children slow down. Alternate hopping on one foot and then the other singing, "Ten Little Indians." Sing the numbers forward, one to ten and then sing backwards. See page 68 if you need the familiar music.

- "Looby Loo" is fun and has lots of movement! See page 66.

Flip Flop the Activity

Divide the group in half. Let one half of the group speak the rhyme like a "Voice Choir" while the other half does the movement. Then flip-flop, or reverse the groups and repeat. See hand signals on page 56.

Pantomime

Let most of the group say a rhyme and choose three or four children at the time to act it out. Take turns.

While Waiting

Read or recite a nursery rhyme or Mother Goose rhyme as "a time filler" in those many spaces in a day when there is not enough time to conduct an entire lesson. Have some of your favorite verses memorized to pull from your professional "bag of tricks" when needed. Smile.

A time filler is not "wasting time"; it is filling time purposefully. Remember Thoreau's adage, "As if you could kill time without injuring eternity." Thus here are some activities for purposeful waiting. Consider a rhyme or verse:

- Waiting for the entire class to arrive such as: Taking turns in the bathroom or at the water fountain.
- To end a class period.
- Waiting for…
- Waiting to…
- Standing in a line to go to the library; back to the classroom; to lunch; or home!

Dramatize

- Act out rhymes simply without props.

- Or provide a single prop for one lesson for interest or emphasis. See page 5 for an example with a Mother Goose doll.

- For an interest center during the year, build a large wooden shoe with laces. Use for this emphasis on nursery rhymes and rhythm. Or get a large empty refrigerator carton from a furniture store and make a cardboard shoe.

Listen to Rhythms in Music

See examples below.

Listen for Certain Sounds in Classical Music

Listen for certain rhythms. Play portions of musical recordings. Tell children what they're listening to hear. You will be training the children's ear to be more discerning, helping them become familiar with portions of classical music, and thus helping them in music appreciation. Listen for enjoyment. Listening can be coordinated with your teaching objectives. Listen for certain sounds. Listen for specific rhythms. Listen for certain instruments of the orchestra. Listen to *parts*, not the work in entirety.

Teachers can listen to music with this idea in mind and hear numerous samples. A few are given. You will "hear" many others.

- Listen for the sound of a man walk-

ing on a tour of Paris in *An American in Paris* by George Gershwin.

- Listen for taxi horns (from the percussion section) in George Gershwin's work "An American Paris."

- Listen for the sound of a donkey's hoofs walking down the trail into Arizona's Grand Canyon in the music "On the Trail" from Grofé's *Grand Canyon Suite*.

- Listen for a certain character played by a specific instrument in Prokofiev's *Peter and the Wolf*. See more in Music, Chapter 5, pages 87–88.

- Does Honegger's "Pacific 231" sound like trains?

Hum, Make Up a Song, Move, and Sway

- Think of a topic and make up a song about anything. Either melody or words first.

- Like Winnie-the-Pooh, hum a little hum (A. A. Milne, 1882–1956).

- Grab your hands in front of you and swing both arms like an elephant trunk.

- Sway your body like a swing and hum a swing song.

- As the children sway like a swing, read or quote the poem "The Swing" from Robert Louis Steven-

son's book of poems, *A Child's Garden of Verses.*

- Rock in a rocking chair and think of a poem or a song. The regular rhythm of the chair will stimulate your thoughts. See "Reading Rocker" pages 33–34.

Rhyme: "Gingerbread Horn"

Some history, a story, and a 5, 4, 4, 4 rhythm to an Early American rhyme.

True Story: In early America "Horn Books" were used in schools. Not a book at all, the paddle held alphabets or papers for school children to read and recite their lessons. At the bottom was a handle. Sometimes cow horn was put over the "little book," thus the name "horn book." Rare today, the horn books were made of various materials: wood, leather, ivory, bone, and even lead.

At Christmastime a special treat for children was a horn made of gingerbread. Eric Sloane researched the legend for a child eating the holiday treat. Note the Old English speech:

"Knowledge is thereby devoured by ye child and a glad yeare with great wealth of learning becomes in store."[24]

Gingerbread Horn

A gingerbread horn
For Christmas morn
To greet the day
When Christ was born!

— Early American rhyme

"A Gingerbread Horn" by Carol O'Regan.

Rhythm of Popping Corn

- Children would enjoy the rhythm of an early American weather rhyme:

"Corn Knee-High
by the Fourth of July!"

- An amusing regional book about corn is Dorothy Van Woerkom's *Tall Corn: A Tall Tale.*[25] The tall Texas tale is not about Jack on a beanstalk but a short little girl on a tall cornstalk. The amusing story and the illustrations by Joe Boddy will be enjoyed by your children. Besides entertaining children there's a definite message about contentment with your height.

- See the riddle "Guess What?" on page 35.

- Several ideas about corn: Pretend to grind corn, p. 76; sing, "Grinding Corn," p. 77; make garlands of popcorn and cranberries for the classroom.

- Teach children to sign "popcorn." Sign language is very expressive and children will be learning another tool of communication (page 59).

Directions: "Hold both "S" hands in front of you with the palms facing up. Flick both index fingers up alternately.[26] See page 59 for popcorn and the complete "Sign Language Alphabet," page 54.

Note: POP-UP, Rise, Appear, and Show-Up are all signed as follows: The right index finger is pushed up between the left index and middle fingers.[27]

- Enjoy *The Popcorn Book* by Tomie de Paola. This non-fiction book has much information about popcorn in the attractive format of de Paola's recognizable art. Be sure to bring an electric popper and a bag of popping corn. Remember at the appropriate times to use all of the senses in your teaching. The smell of popping popcorn is memorable.

- Chant "Grinding Corn," pages 76–77.

Introduce a Book or a Lesson with a Nursery Rhyme

- Recite "A, B, C, D, E, F, G…" to introduce the book *Alphabears.*

- Use other traditional Mother Goose and nursery rhymes to introduce a book or a lesson. Obtain the lovely alphabet book by the Hagues: *Alphabears: An ABC Book* by Kathleen Hague (1984). Each of the bear illustrations by Michael Hague

could be a lovely painting on the wall of a nursery. Each letter of the alphabet has the name of a boy or a girl bear. Use these nursery rhymes:

- Sing the ABC song. See page 46.

- Read or recite the rhyme "What are little boys … girls… made of?" about "Little Boys and Little Girls" on page 11.

- Read *Alphabears*, enjoying the rhythm and the rhyme in each verse and showing children the beautiful bear illustrations as you read.

- If children ask for to hear the story again, re-read. Turn the pages showing the illustrations and let children answer these questions in unison. "Boys, can you name the boy bears? Girls, can you remem-

ber the names of the girl bears? Let's see." You say each letter of the alphabet and see if they remember. Kyle and William, Laura and Vera.

- Say: "This time anyone may answer who can remember the names of the little boy or little girl bears." Then repeat the alphabet, slowly turning the pages.

Reading Rocker

Reading and rocking chairs go together. For a special promotion idea put a rocking chair in your library or classroom. The rhythm of the words with the rocking motion will be enjoyable to you and your students.

How to promote and use the reading rocker? Use these tested ideas:

- **Rocking Chair**. Get a rocking chair. Bring one from home if necessary

"Read and Rock" by Carol O'Regan.

for special emphasis. Look at a garage sale; refinish or paint an old chair. Or plan ahead and put a rocking chair in your library budget.[28] I think a rocking chair is an attractive permanent addition to a library or a classroom.

- **Promotion**. Place a sign on or above your chair, "READING ROCKER" I made a sign like "the two R's" were sitting in the rockers. The alliteration of the "r's" is fun to roll off your tongue. The children will enjoy repeating the phrase too: "Reading Rocker."

- **Read in Rocker**. Reading in the rocking chair was required. My only rule concerning the library reading rocker is that one must be reading while sitting in the chair. Your joy will be to keep some reading material in the chair. With today's world of computers and emphasis on multimedia, the reading emphasis will be enjoyed.

- **"Casey at the Bat"** My first "Reading Rocker" was in an elementary school library in the springtime. I read the poem "Casey at the Bat" to the class, introduced the "Reading Rocker" and explained the one rule: "To enjoy reading while in the chair." The volume of poetry from which I'd read was in the rocker with a bookmark at the verse by Ernest Thayer.

- **Picture Books and Storytime** is another idea for the "reading Rocker." After the spring baseball season my reading rockers had more mileage with the "R's." The furniture had been in the front of the library for the poetry emphasis. I moved the chair to the picture books section for a time of "Recreational Reading." I sat in the rocker during "storytime," then the children took turns reading and rocking. I taught them the meaning of the words, "Recreation Reading"— Reading for Enjoyment — reading for fun!

- **Read Reference.** You can move the rocking chair to create interest. After a few weeks the rocker was moved again, this time to the reference section. A new sign was made to help the children learn the purpose of the chair in the new location. The sign "Read Reference." Another teaching opportunity. Lessons plans including these teaching points. Reference books cannot be checked out. You refer to or look at the books in the library for information or for enjoyment. Teach book care before allowing free use of the reference section. These books are usually very expensive. I found many young children enjoyed the privilege of being in this section of the library and looking at the pictures or reading the reference materials.

Note to Librarians. Reading Reference can be recreation reading! A suggestion for librarians. Teach the children to use their time wisely in the library. When you don't have anything else to read, browse in the reference books for fun. You find interesting information you might not see any other way.

Louisiana Langiappe. (A Creole French term meaning something extra.) The "Reading Rocker" promotion was written for an elementary school library but can be easily adapted to the individual classroom at school or for home use. (Many adults home school their children.)

Budget Item. Consider placing a rocking chair in your school library budget, classroom budget, or home budget. This item can carry you through the school year with promotion for:

1) A "Reading Rocker"
2) A "Reference Rocker"
3) "A Recreational Reading Rocker"

Funny-Silly Riddles and Rhymes

A Riddle

Runs all day and never walks,
Often murmurs, never talks;
It has a bed and never sleeps;
It has a mouth and never eats.
     Answer: A River!
                    — Nursery Rhyme

You may decide to use this nursery riddle as a "Who Am I Riddle?" You need to know your children. There's too much symbolism for very young children to understand the humor or either version. Generally, 2nd and 3rd grade children will enjoy the riddles.

Who Am I?

I run all day and never walk!
I often murmur but never talk!
I have a bed but never sleep!
I have a mouth but never eat!
Who Am I?
    Answer: A River

Guess What?

Corn
Kernels.
Heat!

Pop,
Salt,
Eat!

_ _ _ _ _ _ _!
    Answer: Popcorn!

Help young children set a pretty table for their daily Snacks or a Spring party. See "Setting the Table" (pages 136–137). Use umbrella place cards, napkins, and a flowerpot centerpiece.

For a fun snack serve "Cucumber Flowers" (see directions, page 149). Let the children guess the name of the vegetable before you show them. Read or recite the riddle "What Veggie?"

What Is It? What Veggie?[29]

The outside is green,
But it's not a watermelon.

The inside has small seeds,
But it's not a cantaloupe.

The inside is white,
But it's not a potato.

The shape is l-o-n-g,
But it's not a zucchini.

What is this long vegetable?
Spelled with a "c" sounding like a "q"?

This veggie long and green
With small white seeds?

CU-CUM-BER?
Cucumber? Cucumber!

                    — G.M. Caughman

Nonsense Words and Play

After children have a command of language they enjoy word play with nonsense words and silly sounds. Older fours through age seven enjoy being silly. Just listen to children play and you will hear some of the giggling and fun. Allow some

fun with words, rhythm, rhyme and sounds. "Silly Billy, Silly Tilly" is a phrase you can use in your class as a signal that a boy or girl is being silly or as a clue that "we will now all play for awhile and act silly." Repeat the nursery rhyme "Hickety Pickety" for some fun with children:

Hickety, Pickety

Hickety, pickety, my black hen,

She lays eggs for gentlemen.

Gentlemen come every day

To see what my black hen does lay.

— Mother Goose Rhyme

Old MacDonald Had a Farm

Old MacDonald had a farm,

E-I-E-I-O.

And on this farm he had some chicks

E-I-E-I-O.

With a chick, chick here, and a chick, chick there,

Here a chick, there a chick,

Old MacDonald had a farm,

E-I-E-I-O.

— Traditional Singing Rhyme

Say or Sing as many verses as you wish, changing the animal name and sound. Suggestions: DUCK...quack; TURKEY...gobble-gobble; PIG...oink-oink; HORSE...neigh. Optional: As the children learn the song, repeat all the sounds from earlier verses before the final: EIEIO!

Funny Rhyme

Peas

I eat my peas with honey,
I've done it all my life.
It makes them taste quite funny,
But it keeps them on the knife.

— Anonymous

If All the World Were Paper

If all the world were paper,
And all the sea were ink,
And all the trees were bread and
    cheese,
What would we have to drink?

— Anonymous

Silly, Silly

Silly Billy,

Silly Willie,

Silly, silly.

Silly Tillie,

Silly Millie,

Silly, Silly.

Silly, Really!

— G.M. Caughman

Knock-Knock Jokes

Do you remember the silly "knock-knock jokes"? They were popular when I was in junior high! Some of the jokes are obscure but children can make up their own jokes with "silly nonsense" questions and answers. Young children will enjoy the rhythm and the reception. My all time favorite knock-knock joke is perfect for young children:

Knock, knock.
Who's There?
Who.
Who, Who?
You Think You're
An Owl Don't You!

— G.M. Caughman

Silly Song

Children will remember the musical scale and have fun learning with this silly song, "The Flea Scale."

Directions for Singing

- Begin singing "la" with the sound on "middle C."
- Sing "la-la-la" up the scale from C to D to E to F to G to A to B to C.
- Sing back down again. Use the following words:

"The Flea Scale"[30]
A Scale Song

[Sing up Scale:]

On my toe there is a flea

Now he's crawling up on me

Past my tummy, past my nose

On my head where my hair grows.

[Sing Back down the Scale]

On my head there is a flea

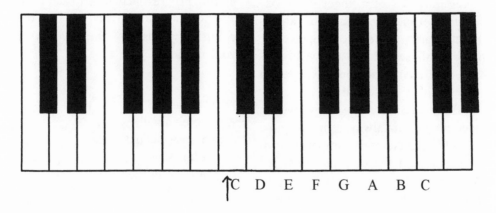

C D E F G A B C

"Middle C" by author.

Now he's crawling down on me

Past my tummy,

Past my knee,

On the floor

Take that you flea."

[Clap hands once!]

Stop Silly

A common expression to explain when children, teens, or even adults get so tickled they laugh and continue to laugh is "your tickle-box is turned over!" You might like to establish a signal as a part of your classroom management such as: "STOP Silly Billy, Silly Tilly. Silly time is OVER!" If a child gets uncontrollably silly or doesn't want to stop when "silly play-time" is over separate them from the rest of the class to rest. Give this instruction: "When you calm down you can rejoin the class."

There is a time to be funny and likewise a time to work. Be firm when it's time to work.

A Time for Everything

"There is a time for everything

A time to LAUGH...

A time to dance...

A time to be silent

and a time to speak."[31]

Finger Plays

Children enjoy the rhyme, rhythm and motions of finger plays. Every teacher needs a "bag of tricks" from which to pull at a moment's notice. What are the purposes of a finger play? Use them for fun and play; relaxation; and as a listening activity. Browse through these rhymes, choose some to try with children, then memorize your favorites to utilize during your school day.

"Here's a Ball" is one of my favorite finger plays. I'm always amazed how much children enjoy the simple rhythm and rhyme and the easy motions. It's easy to remember. Try it now and add to your store of games for recreation and relaxation.

Here's a Ball[32]

Motions: Make three balls in the air, using fingers, hands, and then arms getting progressively larger each time.

Repeat motion on the last three counting words. Use these words with your motions.

Here's a ball,
And here's a ball,
And a great big ball I see.
Are you ready?
Can you count them?
One, two, three!

Open and Shut!

Open, shut them.

Open, shut them.

Give a little clap.

Open, shut them.

Open, shut them.

Put them in your lap.[33]

Motions: Alternate opening fingers and making a fist as words indicate.

Clap hands on the cue of the third line.

Fold hands in lap on last line.

Are You Ready?

(Sing to the tune of "Are You Sleeping?" page 69.

Are you ready?

Are you ready?

Please sit down.

Please sit down.

Time to be quiet.

Time to be quiet.

Hands in lap.

Hands in lap.[34]

This finger play is excellent for quieting young children after recess or as an activity in the classroom. Say or sing "Are You Ready?" See page 73 if you need the music.

Short Counting Rhyme: One Two, Three, Go!

One for the money,

Two for the show,

Three to get ready,

And four to go!

— Traditional Rhyme

Game: Singing Numbers

Use the song "The Mulberry Bush" to sing the game, "Writing Numbers in the Air." Adapt the tune in this way:

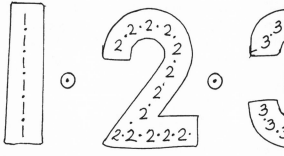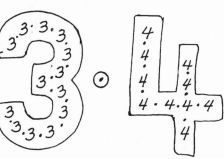

"One, Two, Three, Four, Go!" by the author.

1. See the written music of "The Mulberry Bush" on page 68.

2. Sing the first eight notes of the tune with new words. For the first verse, adapt the first eight notes to the words: "Start at the top and come straight down."

3. Repeat three times.

4. Use the music from the last phrase of "The Mulberry Bush"—"So early in the morning"—changing the words to the number song. For verse one sing: "To make a number one."

5. Adapt remaining words to this tune.

Note: Children often come to school writing their numbers incorrectly. Some children write numbers from the bottom up or from the side. This exercise emphasizes starting at the TOP for each number. Watch the children as you say or sing the numbers. Repeat over and over as necessary: "Start at the top, Kirk." "Start at the top, Lauren."

Writing Numbers in the Air
(Game for Numbers 1–9)
— G.M. Caughman

GAME: SAY THE NUMBER

Instructions: Start the game by saying: "Take your pointer finger as high in the air as you can reach." Say each number distinctly. Write the number in the air with your index finger.

Use this activity for instruction; for a learning game, or for review.

WRITE NUMBERS IN THE AIR

1. Start at the top and come straight down (3X);
To make a number one.

2. Half around and straight across (3X);
To make a number two.

3. Half around and half around (3X);
To make a number three.

4. Down, out, and straight across (3X);
To make a number four.

5. Down, around, and back across (3X);
To make a number five.

6. Curve down, and come around (3X);
To make a number six.

7. Straight across and then slant down (3X);
to make a number seven.

8. Around, down, and back to the top (3X);
To make a number eight.

9. Around, up, and down to the side (3X);
To make a number nine.

Bend and Stretch

Bend and stretch, reach for the stars.
There goes Jupiter, here comes Mars.
Bend and stretch, reach for the sky,
Stand on tip-e-toe, oh, so high![35]

I Clap My Hands

I clap my hands,
I touch my feet,
I jump up from the ground.

I clap my hands,
I touch my feet,
And turn myself around.[36]

Note: Two versions of "Wiggles." Choose your favorite.

The Wiggles

I wiggle my fingers,
I wiggle my toes,
I wiggle my shoulders,
I wiggle my nose.
Now the wiggles are out of me,
And I'm just as still as I can be.[37]

I Wiggle My Fingers

I wiggle my fingers, I wiggle my toes.
I wiggle my shoulders, I wiggle my
    nose.
Now no more wiggles are left in me,
So I will be still, as still as can be![38]

Quiet Time

I've just come in from playing,
As tired as I can be
I'll cross my legs
And fold my hands.
I'll close my eyes
So I can't see.

I will not move my body,
I'll be like Raggedy Ann.
My head won't move,
My arms won't move,
I'll just be still
Because I can.[39]

Shhh!

Shhh … be very quiet.
Shhh … be very still.
Fold your busy, busy hands.
Close your sleepy, sleepy eyes.
Shhh … be very still.[40]

Play with Rhythm in Words on Any Topic!

Play with words. Play with rhythm and rhyme. You can create play with rhythm in sounds and words and rhyme during any day at any time on any topic. Young children at play do this all the time. Enjoy listening to them use word play. Try the following example and others from this book. You can also make up your own!

Corn

Show children an ear of corn. Say, "Corn."

Point to one grain of the corn. Say, "Kernel."

Ask, "What happens if you heat a kernel of corn?"

Give children "think time!" Someone will figure it out!

Say in rhythm (three times): "Heat, eat. Heat, eat. Heat, eat!"

Laugh with the children as they think of the word: Popcorn!

Repeat the riddle rhyme: on page 35. "Corn? Guess What?"

Let children repeat rhyme and solve the riddle.

Lagniappe: Put kernels of corn in an electric popcorn popper.

Enjoy smells! Enjoy eating popcorn together.

Counting Song: Ten Little Indians

Counting rhymes and songs will help children learn number names. With the popularity of television in almost every home, there would be few children, if any, starting school who could not count to ten. But this song is a fun review of the beginning numbers. Through watching and listening to children sing you can learn quickly if your students know how to say the numbers.

Naming is not comprehending what the number represents but it is a start. Holding up the ten fingers one at a time gives a representation of a finger for each number. Watch the children's mouths as you sing or play with this song. For music see page 68. Be sure children correctly pronounce: One, two, three, four, five, six, seven, eight, nine, ten.

Count down! Singing the second verse may be more challenging for children. Counting backwards from ten to one can be done with ease by most children for they have grown up watching space launches. You may hear a cheerful call, "Blast off!" when counting from ten to one. See page 43.

More Finger Plays

Here Are My Ears

Here are my ears,
Here is my nose.
Here are my fingers,
Here are my toes.
Here are my eyes,
Both open wide.
Here is my mouth
With white teeth inside.
Here is my tongue
That helps me speak.
Here is my chin,
And here are my cheeks.
Here are my hands
That help me play
Here are my feet
For walking today.[41]

Growing: Now I Am Four

When I was one, I was so small,
I could not speak a word at all.

When I was two, I learned to talk;
I learned to sing; I learned to walk.
When I was three, I grew and grew.
Now I am four, and so are you.[42]

Sometimes I Am Tall

Sometimes I am tall,
Sometimes I am small
Sometimes tall, sometimes small,
See how I am now?[43]

Touch

I'll touch my hair, my lips, my eyes.

I'll sit up straight and then I'll rise.

I'll touch my ears, my nose, my chin,

Then quietly* sit down again.[44]

*Use three syllables to pronounce "qui-et-ly" for the 8-count rhythm of the rhyme.

Count Buttons

Rich man,

Poor man,

Beggar man,

Thief,

Doctor,

Lawyer,

Merchant,

Chief.

Directions:

- Have children stand with a partner and hold hands.
- Find someone wearing clothes with buttons down the front.
- Count the buttons as you say the rhyme.
- When you run out of buttons, that will one day be your vocation.

Note: A Counting Rhyme. Count the buttons on a shirt or dress. Or bring a jar of buttons from home for children to count. Count the buttons on the back cover of the 2000 Caldecott Award winner (Taback).

Count-Down from 10 to 1

Show children the reproduction of the stamp commemorating the 25th anniversary of the first moon landing. Space technology is a part of every child's life today.

Have the children count backward as in a space launch: 10, 9, 8, 7, 6, 5, 4, 3, 2, 1. Then have them count 10 objects to associate the item with the number.

"25th Anniversary of the Moon Landing" (Stamp design © 1994 U.S. Postal Service. Reproduced with permission. All rights reserved.)

Counting Books

Choose your favorite counting books for children. One of these will surely be *Demi's Count the Animals 1, 2, 3.** Look it up in your library. Buy it for your classes. Ask a parent-teacher organization to buy one for each preschool child.

*Enjoy other books by Demi. Especially: *Demi's Find the Animal ABC* and *Demi's Opposites: An Animal Game Book. Demi's Count the Animals 1,2,3* is also a game book. Enjoy!

- Read aloud the counting rhymes from 1 (One) to 20 (Twenty).

- Let children enjoy counting 100 animals: A large zebra holds 100 tiny zebras; Count to 100 with "Two by Two" animals.

- Count by fives to 100 on a chart of animals.

- 5, 10, 15, 20, 25, 30 … to 100.

- Count by 10's to 100.

- The book is filled with colorful animals doing funny things.

- Many surprises fill this book, including the title page and the dedication page.

- More than a "counting book" the children will be delighted with this title and you will see correlation with your curriculum objectives.

- Animals. There are many funny colorful animals for children to count and enjoy. One most unusual, the pangolin. Other funny animals are: rhino, elephants, ducks, tigers, polar bears, ponies, penguins, kangaroos, rooster, hen, chicks, pigs, koalas, frogs, rabbits, monkeys, giraffes, water buffaloes, snakes, and geese. I've listed them to help you read this book anytime any of these animals are in a story or lesson.

"Count 1, 2, 3" by the author.

America's
ABC
Libraries
XYZ
USA 20c
Legacies To Mankind

4

*Rhythm of the ABC's,
Signs and Signals*

Rhythm of the A, B, C's

You can recite the alphabet in a rhythm so the letters will rhyme. After the beginning letter, stop on the following letters: G, P, V, and Z to hear the rhyme.

A B C D E F G,
H I J K L M N O P,
Q R S T U V
W X Y Z.

The ABC Song

Many versions of this song exist, for like fairy tales it's often passed along in the oral tradition. As a child I was taught the version: "Now I've said my ABC's. Tell me what you think of me." I've also sung this printed version reversing the words, "Shall we be" to sing "Happy we shall be…" Enjoy the old "ABC Song" sung by many generations. Note the caution on p. 47.

1. The version printed below.

2. Near the end, change "shall we be" to: "Happy, happy we shall be…"

3. Near the end, after "Z," sing, "Now I've said my ABC. Tell me what…"

4. Same as #3 except use "sung" in place of "said": "Now I've sung my ABC. Tell me what you think of me."

Sing ABC in Four Versions

Choose Your Favorite from Four Versions of The ABC Song:

A, B, C
–Traditional song

A, B, C, D, E, F, G, H, I, J, K, L, M, N, O, P, Q, R, S, and T, U, V,

W (double you and) X, Y, Z. Hap-py, hap-py shall we be, When we've learned our A, B, C.

Previous page: "ABC XYZ: Americas' Libraries" © 1982 USPS.

The Alphabet

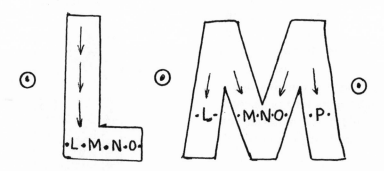

"El-lem" by the author.

Many kindergarten teachers have the Pledge of Allegiance to the Flag, then sing "The ABC Song" and recite the alphabet as a part of their morning classroom routine. You can sing and recite the ABC's, the second time pointing to a chart of alphabet cards posted year-round in the classroom.

However when you review the alphabet with children be sure to listen to their pronunciations of the letters. Be careful yourself to crisply enunciate each letter of the alphabet when you name them one by one. Particularly notice the section, "L, M, N, O, P!" Watch the children's lips. Listen to them sing and say the letters. Help children properly pronounce the letters of the alphabet.

"C's and Q's Veggie Garden"

I learn my ABC's
And Q, R, S, T, U, V's.
Why do some words
Not pronounce their
sound?

CUCUMBER
Does not begin with Q!
The veggie sounds like
Q- come- b-r-r-r!
Brrr, I'm cold. I'm cool.
Cool as a cucumber!

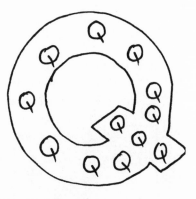

— G.M. Caughman

Alphabet Books

The market is teeming with alphabet books and more are produced annually. Check out a variety from your school and public libraries. Read through the books to choose and use your favorites. I enjoy alphabet books and have bought many for my personal collection. Consider the children you teach and select the best for them.

"Illuminated Letters."

Alphabears: An ABC Book

The Hagues — Michael and Kathleen — did a charming all-bear alphabet book. *Alphabears: An ABC Book* has a rhyme and a bear for each letter of the alphabet. Each of Michael's soft illustrations could hang in a child's nursery. Have a School "Bear Day" and enjoy the book with a class of preschoolers. Bear lovers of all ages will enjoy the book.[45]

Alphabears: An ABC Book. Kathleen Hague. Illustrated by Michael Hague. New York: Holt, Rinehart and Winston, 1984. ISBN: 0-03-062543-2

Flowers

F is for flowers. Read two books about flowers by the Lobels. Arnold and Anita Lobel collaborated on the title *On Market Street*. In this alphabet book the letter "F" is for flowers in a shop on Market Street. An unusual alphabet book with a story, a beginning and an end. The Lobels also collaborated on a cumulative tale. The story begins and ends with the phrase from the title: *The*

"Flower" by Carol O'Regan.

Rose in My Garden. All these lovely flowers are in the garden too: hollyhocks, marigolds, zinnias, daisies, bluebells, lilies, peonies, pansies, tulips, and sunflowers. Both of these books are a delight to share with children. Decorate your desk any time of the year by placing a single fresh flower in a vase.

Nursery Rhymes. Read or recite these flower nursery rhymes: How does your garden grow, "Mistress Mary"? on page 8. The riddle-rhyme "Daffy-Down Dilly" on page 10.

Anno's Alphabet

Mitsumasa Anno has created a most unusual alphabet book, *Anno's Alphabet: An Adventure in Imagination.* In this creative look at the alphabet, each letter appears to be carved from wood. See more about this book in "Challenging Alphabet Books," page 50.[46]

Make an Alphabet Book

Modern children have many sources of information. Consider making an unusual class book and individual books as well. Choose a word for each letter that will be unusual to your children. Consider their age and development and experiences. Make a list as you decide on the pictures for the book. Let the children do research by looking for pictures and information considering their development and using what's available to you: non-fiction library books; classroom books; personal books; computer, Internet; or classroom encyclopedias. As children obtain information, remember: Any level of research *is* research![47] Below is an example of a word for your alphabet book. You think of others as you browse through your dictionary for ideas!

Mint

- A MINT can be a place where money is made.

 is for Mint

"M" by author.

- MINT is also a plant used for flavoring.

- In Early America, MINT was a major farm crop. Almost every home had mint hanging upside down for quick use. Mint was used for tea and medicines. Today it's also used in candy.

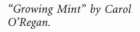

"Growing Mint" by Carol O'Regan.

Challenging Alphabet And Other Books

While you teach the alphabet to some children you can challenge others who know the names of the letters by handing them wonderful books. Many young children have grown up with books in the home and enjoy looking at books independently. You will also enjoy these books with children when appropriate:

- *Anno's Alphabet: An Adventure in Imagination* is truly a unique alphabet book. Created by Japanese artist Mitsumasa Anno, wood is the unifying theme of the book. Each letter of the alphabet appears to be carved from a block of wood. You will want to touch the page to be sure the letters are flat. The subtitle is true: *An Adventure in Imagination*. In this well-crafted book, children must think to solve problems, identify unusual designs in borders, and discover surprises. In *Books for the Gifted Child*, sisters Harris and Baskin give a glowing review of this book. "A perfectly designed book, which reveals new surprises with each rereading. The front dust jacket shows a question mark carved from wood; the back displays the block of wood from which it was carved…. Optical illusions do not follow a pattern and there are no clues pointing to their presence; each must be individually discovered. Artistry and layout are impeccable; the whole effort is a feast for eye and mind."[48]

- *ABC Book of Early Americana*. (Wings Books, 1963). Eric Sloane created an alphabet book for all ages. This text is *not* for very young children and not for all children. Young children interested in the rhythm and beauty of letters and words will enjoy the illustrations. Teachers will enjoy the history of early America, the stories about alphabets, penmanship and the printed letters. Sloane tells several interesting stories about his friend and neighbor, Fred Goudy, the famous type designer. Fascinated with letters, Goudy's research included trips to Greece where he made rubbings of stone letters. While some children learn to say and write their alphabet, other children might enjoy looking at the illustrations of early America in this unusual book. As a teacher, challenge all children, considering the needs of the brightest child for each child is important. A book such as this can be placed in the hands of a curious child. Watch the child to see if the book captures their interest. Give the child opportunity at some point in your day to ask you questions about the images they see. Look for the book in your library.

- David Macaulay. Children interested in building blocks, construction, and architecture can be referred to many of the books by David Macaulay. Though the text is too advanced for young children "the large handsome pen-and-ink sketches are even more important than the text in explaining the problems of the ambitious architectural endeavors."[49] Several books show illustrations of the workman of the period and their tools. Consider your students as you look at Macaulay's wonderful teaching books. See *Cathedral, City, Pyramid, Castle, and Mill.*[50]

- Schoolwide "A to Z." Some schools specialize in lower or upper elementary. If you are in a lower elementary school or a developmental childhood center plan an "A to Z Activity" for one day after lunch. Or plan a "A to Z day" school-wide.

- Use the "Zipper" to make a bookmark to distribute school-wide weeks before the event. Use the caption: "Find the Signs from A to Z." Type in the name of your school.

- Have a faculty committee choose an object for each letter of the alphabet and print the words on heavy cardstock (about 8" × 8").

- Hide the signs about the school. Make an announcement on the public address system in the morning. What the children should watch for during the day, "Signs from A to Z." The child finding the sign takes it to the school office and

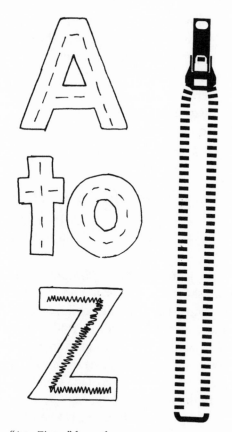

"A to Zipper" by author.

wins a point for his or her homeroom. At the end of the day whoever finds the most gets special school-wide privileges such as extra recess time or ice cream.

Eight Hands Round
A Patchwork Alphabet
by Paul/Winter[51]

- For young children, show illustrations and read the one word for each letter of the alphabet. An interesting introduction to handmade quilts in early America.[52]

- Take a week to read several pages a day. Be sure to show the art.

- Read to first and second graders to gain a fascinating look at the early history of America through twenty-six different patchwork quilt designs.

- Plan to use the introduction to define the term "patchwork."

- Shows many activities and occupations in our early history through the stories in the quilt squares.
- Enjoy much wordplay with the terms square and round in title and text. The book title comes from a square dance "round" after a quilting party. Square dancers often make a circle as they "all join hands and circle left" (usually left, occasionally right).[53] Quilters sew quilt squares but sit around the quilting square frame. Square dancers dance in "squares" formed by four couples. Often they join hands to make a circle.

Teaching with Eight Hands Round

A PATCHWORK ALPHABET
Ann Paul and Jeanette Winter

1. September. For "Grandparents Day," show the "G" page and read the text. Show the fans. Let children each make a simple accordion fold fan of paper. School gift for grandparents: Obtain fans made in China from variety stores. Have a display of fans from faculty in the school library.

Discuss with children: Do you use a hand fan? Discuss the purposes and use of fans in the early days of our country. Remember, no air conditioning then!

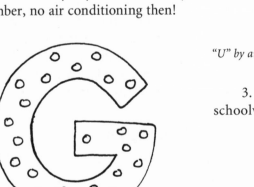

"G" by author.

2. February. During "Black History Month" in February, introduce the term "Underground Railroad" by reading only the "U" page. The term referred to people, not a railroad.

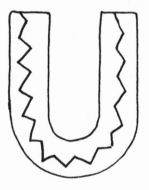

"U" by author.

3. March. In preparation for a schoolwide "Kite Flying Day" in the

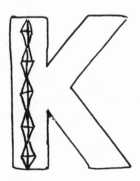

"K" by author.

windy month of March, read the "K" page. Ask children: "Can you see the kites in the quilt designs?"

1. September — "Grandparents Day," read the "G."

2. February — "Black History Month," show the "U."

3. March — For a schoolwide "Kite Flying Day," read the "K" page.

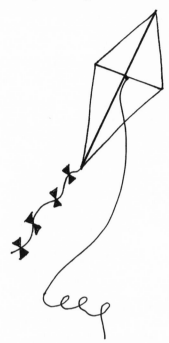

"March Kite" by author.

For older or more mature children, supply them with graph paper and encourage them to design a kite or a quilt.

Place a paper bookmark in these places in *Eight Hands Round: A Patchwork Alphabet* by Ann Paul and Jeanette Winter:

"Bookmark Contest."

Sign Language, Signals and Signs

American Sign Language

I believe learning the "manual alphabet" is a basic skill for an educator and a citizen in our society. You can learn to fingerspell the alphabet — just practice. Then teach the children in your classroom or library. Let "singing" be fun. Young children enjoy learning sign language. Sign language is one of the most used languages in the United States. You may have children in your school, library, or home who are hard-of-hearing or have a hearing impair-

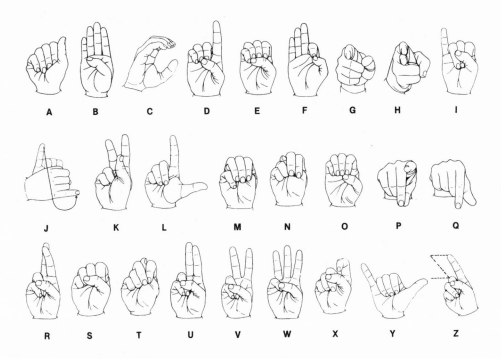

The Manual Alphabet (reprinted by permission of Gallaudet University Press).

ment. It's interesting that the sign for the word "deaf" combines the signs for ear plus closed. The statistics of our population with a hearing loss are astounding — in America over 20 million people.[54]

Sign with Enthusiasm

Enthusiasm is essential in communicating with the hearing-impaired. "Facial expression is extremely important when signing to the deaf. The deaf person relies heavily upon the combination of facial expressions, body language, and speaking or mouthing the words to be sure to include these as you sign."[55]

A personal illustration of this essential point. One of my teachers in a signing music class was teaching us the word "amazing" and had emphasized the importance of using facial expression when signing. "Use both hands and make V's by your eyes at the temple," she

said. When we opened our fingers to make the V's each class member also opened her eyes widely as we signed the word "amazing." It was exaggerated and funny. Funny because we naturally gave expression to the word!

My interest has been life-long. My first serious attempts to learn to sign were prompted by meeting a young friend at "The Y" exercise class. So few were trying to communicate with her. A woman in the class was a special education teacher and began a small class. My insistence that you learn to finger spell the alphabet grew from this experience. Roz and I often communicated in sign but she is such an excellent lip reader and my signing is so slow that I mostly used short-cut words I'd learned or that she taught me. When she didn't understand my "new language," I'd spell it out and she cheerfully and patiently "listened." So many words are based on the manual alphabet. The alphabet made it possible for us to communicate any word. Please learn to finger spell the alphabet.

I believe the beauty, grace, and expressiveness of signing and the desire of many to better communicate with the hearing impaired are helping the deaf to enter the mainstream of society. This beautiful silent language is eloquent in its simplicity and has become a popular art form for drama, music, and theater.

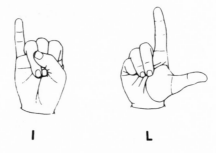

"A.S.L."

The sign for "I love you" combines the ASL (American Sign Language) "I" and the "L" to form one sign, "I love you." Teach ALL of your children to make this sign. Each will be able to communicate the most important phrase to the hearing impaired. Remind the children that the words must be backed up by honest actions. Don't sign nor say the words unless you mean them. Words in sign language are still words, just in another form.

American Sign Language: "I Love You." (Stamp design © 1993 U.S. Postal Service. Reproduced with permission. All rights reserved.)

The Rhythm of Hand Signals

1. **Choral Speaking.** I've worked out these hand signals and have used them with groups of children. You may choose to make up different signals. The main thing is to decide on a set of signs and use them consistently with the children.

Hand Signals for Choral Speaking

Thumb extended to the right side = girls speak.

Two fingers moved to the left side = boys speak.

One finger straight up = solo voice.

Five fingers extended straight ahead, palm up = unison.

(Unison means all voices together.)

Notes: Using hand signals will help save your voice. Also using the same hand signals throughout the year helps the child feel comfortable in their school surroundings. Consistency as a teacher develops an expected response from the children. Children like boundaries, guidelines, and knowing what is expected.

Mark Time or Count Time

2. **Mark Time.**

- Read or recite a rhythmic poem out loud to yourself. Tap your fingers in rhythm as you read. Repeat. Notice the regular rhythm. Which pattern is the poem most like? Choose one: 1-2, 1-2; OR 1, 2, 3, 1, 2, 3; OR 1, 2, 3, 4; 1, 2, 3, 4.

- Notice the patterns for you to beat time or mark time. This is how to direct music. Practice waving your hand up and down in these patterns, repeating, 1-2, or 1-2-3, or 1-2-3-4.

- Practice alone in front of a mirror until you are comfortable waving your hands in the air. Hint: Try to move your wrists and not flap your elbows.

- After you become comfortable marking time, you can use the illus-

trations of the different time patterns and practice again.

- Try your new skill on a group of children. With practice, you will enjoy this activity and find it a useful aid in your teaching.

- Application: Use these hand signals for directing groups of children in saying rhymes, poems, choral readings or leading music.

Need help? Do you need more help in understanding what the fractions mean? 2/4, 3/4, and 4/4: These numbers are called a time signature. They refer to the number of beats in a measure. Also they designate what kind of note gets how many counts. For example: In common time, 4/4 (like a march rhythm), the quarter note gets one count. For more complicated directing, get help from the school band or choral director or a church musician. Also check the Music section, 780, of your school or public library.

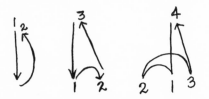

"Directing" by author.

3. **Hand Signals** to show feelings. You can teach children to indicate their feelings to you without a word by these hand signals. Adults do this with a shrug of the shoulders or other gestures. These suggested hand signals for children are more descriptive and give you a quick gauge of the children's feelings. Use the information at other times during the school day to talk to the children about their feelings. Help the children learn how to use this information to share with each other and express care for one another. Children can early show compassion and learn to encourage each other. You can really listen to the children's deep needs. Help them learn to handle their emotions in appropriate ways. Occasionally you may need to refer a child to the school counselor for more

help. Depending on your teacher-pupil ratio, give individual attention, as you are able. Encourage the children to look for the positive in each new day. They have the opportunity to meet the challenges of a new day, as do you.

Instructions. The teacher will say: "Use your right or left hand to show me how you feel today."

1. "Are your feelings very high, like this?"

(Hold hand up high above head.)

2. "Or are your feelings very low today?"

(Hold hand way down as far as you can.)

3. "Or are your feelings somewhere in between?"

(Hold hand back and forth in the middle, about shoulder level.)

Teach children the indicators as follows:

- Hand high: Feelings are great, happy, glad, terrific, joyful

- Hand low: Feelings are sad, bad, terrible, awful, gloomy

- Hand in between: Feelings are pleasant, contented, satisfied, O.K.

Signals and Signs

As a part of your classroom management you may choose to use some of these hand signs to signal to the children an immediate need to watch you, the teacher, and listen for further instructions.

1. **Freeze**. Raise your right arm above the head. Extend five fingers of right hand straight up. As each child sees "the signal," they can be trained to duplicate the signal and freeze in their tracks. It will become like a game for the children. An added benefit would be during

fire drills or other times when you would be responsible for the safety of the children you can get their attention quickly.

2. **Silence.** Raise your right index finger across lips forming the sound, "Sh-h-h." This familiar signal still works.

3. **Flick the Lights.** Some teachers use the lights as a signal to be quiet. Occasional use for discipline would be effective if the device were not overused. I prefer to use the "Freeze" technique mentioned above. There are many times a light switch might not be available. (Examples: Outside at recess when you need to get the children's attention immediately. Or in a situation when the electricity is off.)

Some Signs You Can Use as Signals

Learn signs for several basic words in sign language and use them in your library or classroom to communicate. Another benefit is that you will be giving the children another tool with which to communicate with the deaf. Several signs:

- Yes: Hold the right "S" hand facing forward and nod the hand up and down. Just like nodding your head!

- No: Bring the right thumb and the index and middle fingers together as if you were pinching the air.

- Lunch: Combine the signs for eat plus noon. Eat is to point to the mouth.

- Bathroom, Restroom and Toilet are all signed as Toilet. "Shake The right 'T' hand in front of the chest with the palm facing forward. Restroom can also be signed by pointing the right 'R' hand forward and moving it in a short arc to the right."[56]

Hints for Using Sign Language

I have taken two sign language classes plus one for signing music. Two of my teachers have emphasized these same three key points:

1) Remember to sign with your palm facing outward toward the deaf person. If you turn the sign toward you it's like talking to yourself![57]

2) Signs are usually made in an area making imaginary lines from head to waist and shoulder to shoulder.

3) Do not bounce your hand. Try to sign your letters in smooth movements to enable deaf persons to better understand.

Music

Music has some different rules. Signing to music is very beautiful and extremely expressive. Many of the words are held for a longer time than in conversation but since most deaf persons cannot hear the music, signing to music can be big and bold and exaggerated. (Note: Rules for music are just the opposite of what I stated above in #3. But I'm sure you see the justification for each.)

Food Words in Sign Language

Teach all of your students these three fun food words:

• Hamburger

• Pizza

• Popcorn

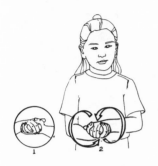  

Left: *Sign language for hamburger.* Middle: *Sign Language for pizza.* Right: *Sign language for popcorn.* From Come Sign with Us, *Jan C. Hafer and Robert M. Wilson. Washington, D.C.: Gallaudet University Press, 1996, pages 94, 98–100. Used by permission.*

5

Rhythm and Rhyme in Singing

Music for Mother Goose Rhymes

Many of the Mother Goose rhymes have traditional melodies that have been passed down from generation to generation. Sing and play many of these games and see which are the favorites of your students. Most of the children will come to school knowing some of these rhymes or songs. Which are your favorites?

Note: The music for "Baa! Baa Black Sheep" starts out like "The ABC Song" but then the rhythm changes. You could adapt these words to the melody of "The ABC Song" if you like. I prefer to sing this song repeating the first line as the ending thus finishing with a positive (the bags full of wool) rather than the negative (penalizing the little boy). See "Mother Goose Rhymes" Chapter 1, pages 10–11.

"Sing with Love" by Carol O'Regan.

Baa! Baa! Black Sheep

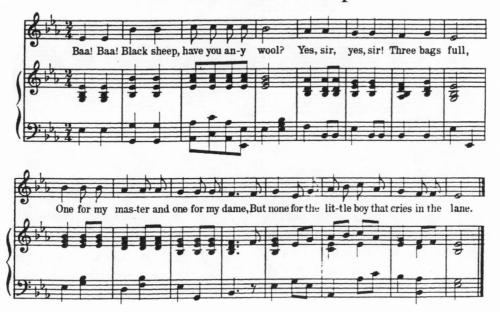

Baa! Baa! Black sheep, have you an-y wool? Yes, sir, yes, sir! Three bags full,

One for my mas-ter and one for my dame, But none for the lit-tle boy that cries in the lane.

Previous page: *"Rhythm in Singing" by Carol O'Regan.*

Mary's Lamb

When you sing "Mary Had a Little Lamb" be sure to add the two stanzas about the lamb following Mary to school. See text in "Mother Goose Rhymes," page 11. These verses are the favorites of children for several reasons:

- Children love animals.
- The lamb evidently broke a school rule of no animals or pets at school.

- It's fun to sing because of the rhythm and rhyme.

Note: In modern schools animals and pets ARE allowed as guests for a special treat or to go with a lesson topic. Learn about sheep and lambs. Arrange for a pet lamb to visit your school.

Traditional song.

Pussy Cat

Children's most common pets are dogs and cats. They love to talk about their pets. Let children sing and act out this song. Choose someone to play the cat who has observed a cat's movements and characteristics.

Actions: Assign three parts:

1. The queen of England sits on her throne in London.

2. The narrator asks questions of the cat.

3. The cat proudly sits listening and answering questions all the while licking and pruning her fur.

Note: I learned the song: "I've Been to London to Visit the Queen." If you sing this version, vary the rhythm of the music to match.

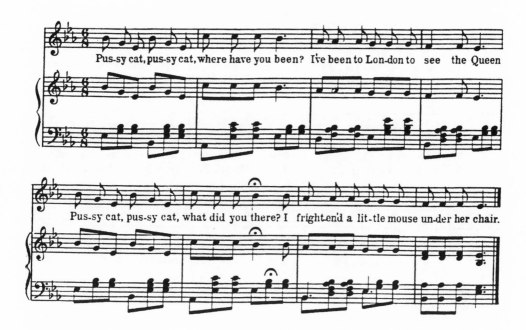

Pus-sy cat, pus-sy cat, where have you been? I've been to Lon-don to see the Queen

Pus-sy cat, pus-sy cat, what did you there? I fright-en'd a lit-tle mouse un-der her chair.

Traditional song.

Twinkle, Little Star

One of the ever-popular childhood songs has a familiar first verse. Perhaps the second verse is new to you. The sun is gone for the stars to be visible. The phrase "When he [referring to the sun] nothing shines upon" is a bit contrived to make a rhyme. Some versions of this nursery rhyme ask: "How I Wonder Where You Are?" which is a different question from: "How I Wonder What You Are?"

- What is the makeup of a star?

- How far away are the stars?

- Can I really wish upon a star?

- How is a star like a diamond?

- Can you define star?

- What does a star look like?

Teaching suggestions: Sing for fun while enjoying the rhythm and rhyme. Or use the song in early elementary classes to introduce a science lesson on space, the sun, stars, or the planets.

Bartlett's (page 449) lists the Taylors as authors of this familiar song: "The Star," 1806 from *Rhymes for the Nursery* by Ann Taylor (1782–1866) and Jane Taylor (1783–1824).

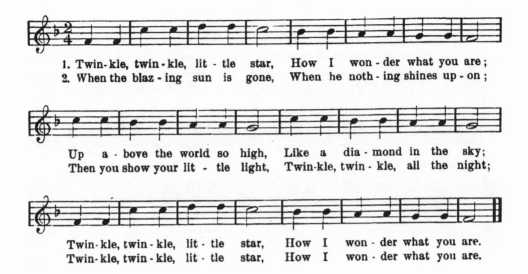

1. Twin-kle, twin-kle, lit-tle star, How I won-der what you are;
2. When the blaz-ing sun is gone, When he noth-ing shines up-on;

Up a-bove the world so high, Like a dia-mond in the sky;
Then you show your lit-tle light, Twin-kle, twin-kle, all the night;

Twin-kle, twin-kle, lit-tle star, How I won-der what you are.
Twin-kle, twin-kle, lit-tle star, How I won-der what you are.

by Ann and Jane Taylor, 1806.

The Farmer in the Dell

Children do not have to know the meaning of a dell to sing and play this old childhood game. But you should know for the one child who might ask you. (A small wooded valley.)

Game Directions: Have the children join hands to form a circle. Choose one child to be the farmer who stands in the center. As each successive verse is sung, the child in the center chooses another from the circle to join them. Finally on the last verse the cheese stands alone in the center. The game begins again as "the cheese" becomes "the farmer" and the game repeats.

Music: Young children can learn the first verse as an Autumn song during a Farm emphasis or lesson on planting and harvesting. Kindergarten, first and second graders will enjoy playing the game with all of the verses. Two versions of the music are given. One version has one flat (B Flat, version #1 next page); the other has one sharp (F Sharp, version #2 next page).

Singing Game: Looby Loo

The singing game "Looby Loo" can become quite active and is good to give energetic children a physical activity that's funny. Preschoolers through grade one particularly enjoy this game. The basic music is given below. Many verses can be added. Begin song by forming a circle. Sing and act out motions for these verses. Each time "Looby Loo" is sung, join hands and march to the center of the circle holding all hands up. Back to the circle, drop hands, and join in these motions:

#1:

4. The child takes the nurse, etc.
5. The nurse takes the dog, etc
6. The dog takes the cat, etc.

7. The cat takes the rat, etc.
8. The rat takes the cheese, etc.
9. The cheese stands alone, etc.

#2:

Traditional singing game.

1. "Put your right hand in … out; … shake, shake, shake, And turn yourself about." Repeat the first two lines after each stanza.

2. "Left hand…"

3. "Both hands."

4. "Right foot."

5. "Left foot."

6. "Head in. Head out."

7. "Right hip."

8. "Left hip."

9. "Whole self" (this is the funniest one!).

Note: Before I could read, I learned a different version of "Looby Loo." Consider this one which I prefer: After you "put your right hand in" each time, you "*take* your right hand out" rather than "put in and put out" as the printed version reads. Both are given for you to choose your preference.

Here we dance Loo-by Loo___ Here we dance loo-by light___

Here we dance Loo-by Loo___ All on a Sat-ur-day night.___

Put your right hand in, Put your right hand out, Then

give your right hand a shake, shake, shake, And turn your-self a-bout.

Traditional singing game.

Song: Oats, Peas, Beans and Barley Grow

"Do you or I know how oats and beans and barley grow?" The wondrous process of growth is explored in this nursery rhyme. For more of a challenge for your tongue, substitute the word "peas" for the word, "and" in the song. As a preschooler that's the version I learned many, many years ago. "Oats, peas, beans, and barley grow." It's fun to try to get all the words in with the music. Good practice on enunciation too!

The music is given here. For three more stanzas, a singing game and a dance, see page 24 of Chapter 2.

Oats and Beans and Barley Grow

1. Oats and beans and bar - ley grow; Oats and beans and bar - ley grow;

Do you, or I, or a - ny one know How oats and beans and bar-ley grow?

"Oats, peas, beans..." Can you sing in rhythm? Traditional Singing Game.

Ten Little Indians

Sing numbers. With the popularity of television in almost every home, there would be few children, if any, starting school who could not count to ten. But this song is a fun review of the beginning numbers. Through watching and listening to children sing you can learn quickly if your students know how to say the numbers.

Naming is not comprehending what the numbers represent. Holding up ten fingers, one at a time, gives a representation of a finger for each number. Watch the children's mouths as you sing or play with this song. Check proper pronuciation of numbers.

Count with singing. Use the melody for "Ten Little Indians" to count any ten things substituting other words for "Indians" and "boys and girls." Sing as you count people, objects, animals, or flowers. Add words as needed to complete the thythm such as "Nine copper pennies now."

1. One lit - tle, two lit - tle, three lit - tle In - dians, Four lit - tle,
2. Ten lit - tle, nine lit - tle, eight lit - tle In - dians, Seven lit - tle,

five lit - tle, six lit - tle In - dians, Seven lit - tle, eight lit - tle,
six lit - tle, five lit - tle In - dians, Four lit - tle, three lit - tle,

nine lit - tle In - dians, Ten lit - tle In - dian boys. (*girls.*)
two lit - tle In - dians, One lit - tle In - dian boy. (*girls.*)

Traditional counting song.

Here We Go Round the Mulberry Bush

Here we go round the mulberry bush,
The mulberry bush, the mulberry bush,
Here we go round the mulberry bush,
So early in the morning.

— Nursery Rhyme

Children enjoy joining hands and moving in a circle as they sing and play this old nursery rhyme. Music is given here for the beginning of the singing game "The Mulberry Bush." This first verse may be enough for very young children. For more verses and two versions of the singing game see pages 24–25 in Chapter 2.

1. Here we go round the mul - ber - ry bush, The mul - ber - ry

bush, the mul - ber - ry bush; Here we go round the

mul - ber - ry bush, So ear - ly in the morn - ing.

Traditional childhood game.

Are You Sleeping?
ONE MELODY: FOUR SONGS!

1. Are You Sleeping? Sing words as shown on music below.

2. Are You Sleeping? This song may be sung as a three- or four-part round. Divide class into three or four parts. See numbers above the music. Each part should stop after singing through the music three times.

3. Bells are Ringing
Bells are ringing!
Bells are ringing!
Children sing.
Children sing.
Merry, merry Christmas!

Merry, merry Christmas!
Bright New Year!
Bright New Year!
    See page 75 for holiday ideas with this version of the song.

4. French Folk Song. The French folk song "Frère Jacques" is sung to this tune.

"Frère Jacques"

Frè-re Jac-ques, Frè-re Jac-ques,
Dor-mez-vous? Dor-mez-vous?
Son-nex lez ma-tin-es, Son-nez les ma-tin-es, Din, Din, Don. Din, din, don.
    — French Folk Song

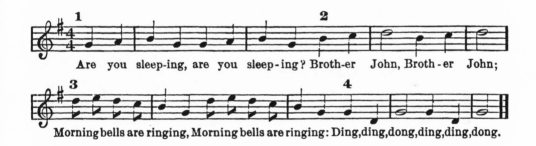

Classic round.

Action Rhyme: Music at Our House

Suggestions:

• Have children act out the motions of the rhyme. Give directions with hand signals as suggested on page 56.

• First read the rhyme to the children. Give them a listening question, such as: "Why is the title of this rhyme 'Music at Our House'?" or

"What instruments are being played in the home in this rhyme?" "Can you imagine how the instruments sound?"

• Let each child choose an instrument they will pretend to play. Read the rhyme again and let all of the children play their instrument.

• Repeat the rhyme letting the girls play the violins, the boys play the flutes and all blow (or toot) horns! The action rhyme:

"Music stickers."

Little brother plays the horn
Toot, toot, toot, toot, toot.

Music at Our house[58]

Mother plays the violin,
Daddy plays the flute,

How I Love to Sing

Sing! Do you like to sing? I do. Whether or not you do, try this song. This will be a favorite of children. Chord markings are given so you or the children can strum an autoharp or guitar as you sing. Enjoy the song about singing.

ELLEN EASTIS

Why?

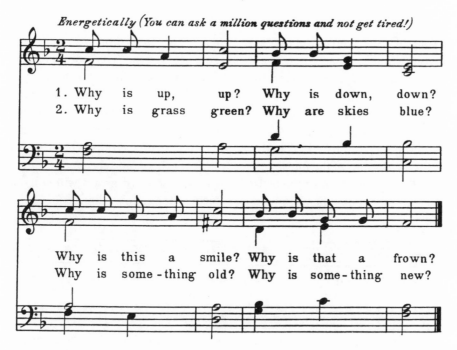

Energetically (You can ask a million questions and not get tired!)

1. Why is up, up? Why is down, down?
2. Why is grass green? Why are skies blue?

Why is this a smile? Why is that a frown?
Why is some-thing old? Why is some-thing new?

I Wonder Why

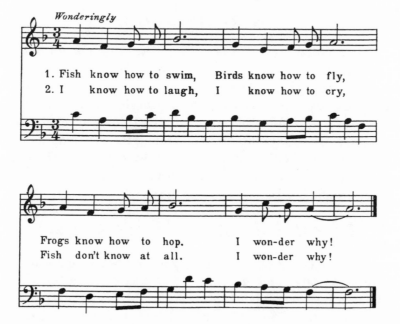

Wonderingly

1. Fish know how to swim, Birds know how to fly,
2. I know how to laugh, I know how to cry,

Frogs know how to hop. I won-der why!
Fish don't know at all. I won-der why!

Lovely Evening

Encourage the children to sing this lovely song of a lovely evening in a soft lovely voice. Smile! That repetition of "lovely" was to make a point. Children can enjoy this simple song. Try it. I remember loving this soft enchanting song in classroom music in grade school.

Teaching Suggestions: Alert children to listen to the rhythm of the music. Ask: "Can you hear the rhythm of the bells?" Sway back and forth like the clapper in a bell. Sing the last words: "Ding! Dong!" with staccato (short, distinct breaks) notes, letting the "NG" sound resonate in your head. Children will have fun prolonging the "ding, dong." Learn the song first. Later the children would enjoy the song as a round. Designate three groups. Cue in the three groups when they should start. Each group repeats the song three times. The third group will sing alone: "Ding, dong, ding, dong."

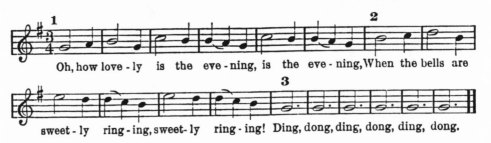

Oh, how love-ly is the eve-ning, is the eve-ning, When the bells are sweet-ly ring-ing, sweet-ly ring-ing! Ding, dong, ding, dong, ding, dong.

Autumn Leaves

A waltz is in a rhythm of 1, 2, 3, perfect for ballet dancers, ballerinas, or dancing leaves (see page 73 for music). Some of Tchaikovsky's *Nutcracker* is in the ¾ rhythm of waltz music. The song "Autumn Leaves Are Now Falling" is in a slow watlz rhythm. The "Tra, la, la's" in the music are especially fun for children twirling around like leaves.

Activity: Obtain red, yellow, and brown pieces of material, each one-yard square. As the children pretend to be dancing leaves, let them take turns waving the colored material over their heads, around their shoulders, or tied around their waists.[59] Note: This could be a colorful feature for parents at the beginning of school.

French Folk Song: "Frère Jacques"

Our world is getting smaller and smaller with jet travel and Internet linkup. We must learn more about people from other countries. Show children the large book *People* by Peter Spier.[60] While noticing ways we are different also point out ways we are alike. Louisiana and other states have exchange programs with "sister cities" in France. Teach your children this French folk song and music from other countries. Note: The ending is different here than on page 69.

Frè - re Jac - ques, Frè - re Jac - ques, Dor-mez-vous? Dor-mez-vous? Son-nez les ma - tin - es,

Son-nez les ma - tin - es, Din, Din, Don   Din, Din, Don.   Din, Don, Din, Don, Don.

Autumn Leaves Are Now Falling

Slow Waltz

Au - tumn leaves are now fall - ing; Red and yel - low and
Au - tumn leaves from the tree tops Flut - ter down to the
Au - tumn leaves when they're tired, In a soft hud - dled

brown; Au - tumn leaves are now fall - ing, See them flut - ter - ing down.
ground, When the wind blows his trump - et, They go whirl - ing a - round.
heap, At the foot of the old tree, Soon will fall fast a - sleep.

Chorus

Tra, la, la, la, la, la, la, Tra, la, la, la, la, la, Tra, la, la, la, la, la, la, la, Tra, la, la, la, la, la.

Oh Where, Oh Where Has My Little Dog Gone?

Teacher, ask: "Who has a puppy, a dog, or a cat?" You will immediately hear many stories. Allow children to express their feelings about owning, caring for and losing their beloved pets. Ask: "Has anyone's pet ever run away?"

My family has had many pets, and my grown daughter works at the Louisiana State University Veterinary School. We've had goldfish, turtles, dogs, and cats. Our oldest pet, our cat Bob, is now 16 years old. See how easy it is to talk about pets.

Sing this song through for the children. Ask them questions:

- What is happening in this song?
- Can you tell about the missing pet from the description in the song?
- How does the song make you feel?
- Have you ever felt sad about a pet?
- Would you like to sing with me?

Sing a phrase at the time, letting children repeat after you.

Variation: I learned the last phrase of the song differently from the following version. Consider this phrase to fit the music better. Instead of "Oh where, Oh where is he?" use: "Oh where, oh where can he be?"

Activities with Music and Singing

1. Celebrate Music Month in March or anytime.

2. Play a tape or compact disc of trumpeter Wynton Marasalis. In 1983, he was the first artist to receive Grammy Awards in both classical and jazz categories in the same year.

3. Obtain "Rondo in C" by Beethoven. Play Beethoven's music as you prepare to read Paul Fleischman's *Rondo in C*. Begin by holding the book with the book jacket facing the children showing a girl playing the piano. Ask: "Does anyone know what's happening in this picture? Yes, can you tell what the girl is doing? Listen." Begin to play the music. Listen yourself. Then stop the music and say: "As I read this story, see if you can tell what is happening." Begin music again, this time very soft as background music as you read the story. Turn the pages toward the children so they can enjoy the soft pastels by Janet Wentworth. After reading, ask, "What is happening in the story?" Discuss the story with the children, listening to their ideas.

4. Lagniappe: After reading *Rondo in C* (Fleischman), let the children paint to the music, "Rondo in C" by Beethoven.

5. Play Tchaikovsky's "The Nutcracker Suite" over the school "public address system" so children can hear the music as they get off the school bus.

6. Before Christmas holidays follow up the introduction to Tchaikovsky in the library or classroom with specific selections from "The Nutcracker Suite." Each day of one week as the classes come into the library, introduce children to the name of the composer and various parts of the music. See pages 91–92.

7. During December and early January, wear a bell on a ribbon around your neck. Teach the children the song "Bells Are Ringing," page 69. Read *The Polar Express*, by Chris Van Allsburg.

8. School supply houses have many delightful stickers with music notes, music symbols (treble clef, bass clef) and pictures of musical instruments. Buy some of these to use throughout the year when you are emphasizing music. For addresses see appendix B, page 161.

9. Daily sing "The ABC Song" with preschoolers and kindergarten children. By repetition they will learn to *say* their alphabet. You can teach the children to associate the sound of the letter with each written letter of the alphabet.

10. Obtain the music for Prokofiev's *Peter and the Wolf*. Prepare the children to hear the classical work by telling them the part of the instruments. Are there any musicians on faculty or musically talented parents with instruments? Arrange for children to see the actual instruments or at least pictures. Look in library books for pictures. See information and other suggestions on pages 87–88.

Traditional childhood song, page 74.

11. Read the true story of the Russian musician Prokofiev on page 87. Learn the story in your own words. Pretend to be young Prokofiev. Tell the story in first person. Do you have a Russian hat to wear? Can you borrow one?

12. Find the silhouette of a music note. See Illustration on page 77. Make one to show the children when you tell the story about Prokofiev's drawings.

13. Paint or draw to the musical fairy tale "Scheherazade" by Rimsky-Korsakoff. See more on page 90.

14. Play the famous overture from Rossini's opera *William Tell* (1829), familiar to teachers from the old black-and-white TV show *The Lone Ranger*. Perhaps classic movie reruns have made the music familiar to today's children.

15. Read *The Paper Crane* by Molly Bang (N.Y.: Greenwillow, 1985). Attractive paper sculptures enhance an old Japanese folktale. A paper crane magically comes to life and dances. Try this idea: In reading the story, stop as the man puts the flute to his lips. Whistle the introduction to *Peter and the Wolf*. Enjoy!

16. Lagniappe: In the music *Peter and the Wolf* the flute plays the part of the bird. (See more about the music on page 87.) For something extra with this book, prepare to play part of the music, setting your tape or disc ready to play the part of the bird. Then read the book. At the end of the story when the man plays the instrument and the bird dances, play the music. Do not add any words to the end of the story, just play music and watch the faces of the children. After the music stops listen to their reactions.

17. Enjoy reading the delightful story to your classes: *Miranda* by Tricia Tusa (Macmillan, 1985). Miranda knows what she likes. And she loves best of all to play the music of Bach, Haydn, and Mozart. But one day something happens to change her life. Miranda hears a one-man jazz band. This book was one of my favorites the year I participated in the International Reading Association's "Children's Choices Project."[61]

18. *A Child's Life in Song* is an original music book the musicians Claude and Carolyn Rhea wrote for situations and events while raising their preschoolers. My two children learned these songs while growing up. Some of the delightful song titles for preschoolers through grade two are: Bubbles, "Why?" (page 71), "At Thanksgiving Time," "The Christmas Star," "Story Time," "I Wonder Why" (page 71), "Mr. Thunder You Can't Scare Me," "Playing House," "Tooth Song," "The Barber Shop," "I Helped My Daddy Pull the Weeds," "Swing Song," "Shaving," "I Can Unbutton a Button."[62]

19. Rhythm: "Grinding Corn"
Indian Chant[63]: Have children sit in a circle and pretend to grind corn while singing this chant. Try this:

The Melody:

E, G, G.
E, D, C.
E, G, G.
E, D, C.

The Words:

"Grinding Corn
Grinding Corn
We are all Grinding Corn."
(Repeat)

Directions:

1.) Sit at piano. Look at keyboard. 2.) Find the "Middle C" on keyboard. 3.) Put thumb on middle C. 4.) Put fifth finger on G. 5.) Rest fingers on notes C, D, E, F, G. 6.) Begin playing with the third finger. See Melody. 7.) Hit keys and play E, G, G. Then E, D, C. Sing the Words. 8.) Repeat chant and act out motions.

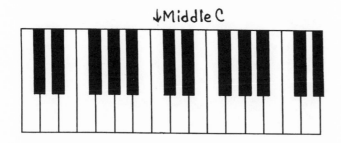

↓Middle C

Part of Piano Keyboard by the author.

20. Music Note. Many products can now be purchased with outlines of all types of objects, music symbols included. Many school systems have paper machines to punch out shaped objects. I still like to hand-cut some objects with paper and scissors. This music note is given with some suggestions for use:

- Name Tags. Use music notes as name tags in kindergarten or first grade.

- Decorate. Cut out music notes to decorate a poster or a bulletin board about a composer, a music book, or the words of a song.

- Program Favors. Make music note name tags or just "favors" for a parents program or a band or chorus concert.

- Shelf Labels. Place a tape curl[64] on the backs of several music notes and attach to the Non-Fiction book shelves in 780 where the music books are located.

- Game. Cut out music notes in primary colors, red, yellow, and blue, and secondary colors, green orange, and violet. Write the color words on the appropriate note. Give out to children randomly.

Use these music notes as a game for the rhyme: "What Color?" Say the words in a sing-song rhythm. See Chapter 8, page 111. The Game: Children are to give their colored note to any child wearing that color when the color word is named that they are holding.

"Music note" by the author.

Motions of Time-Tested Songs:

1. "I'm a Little Teapot." Motions: Two hands, one on hip as a handle; one stuck out as the teapot spout.

2. "Where Is Thumbkin?" Motions: Thumbs wave to each other as do each of successive fingers. At the end of each verse, they "run away" behind your back.

3. "Eency Weency Spider." Motions: Use two hands. Move thumb to index finger over and over. Fingers like rain. Both hands use sweeping motion. Form large sunshine. Start spider climbing again with thumb and index finger.

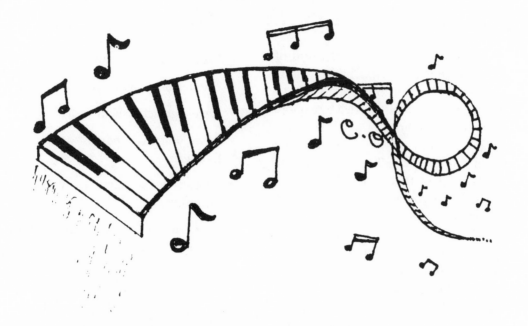

6

Rhythm of Music

The Rhythm of Music

Introduce the wonderful world of music to your children. Children enjoy rhythm. Daily add music naturally to your classroom. I was startled by a quote from an old school book.[65] Teachers taught all subjects in schools in the beginning of the 1900s. The quote is meaningful in that context as well as today. See if you agree with the strong statement:

"Music is the most powerful vitalizing factor the teacher can use in the daily work." Furthermore, the author stated a purpose in language that may sound flowery, but listen to the emotion of the quote: "The songbook is an appeal to the school teachers of America to introduce the sunshine of music into the hearts and souls of the youth of the country."[66]

Certainly music can enrich life. Utilize the rhythm and beauty of music in your classroom this year.

Experience the Rhythm of Music

- Play a xylophone or a zither;

- Paint or dance to music.

- Use sign language to express a song.

- Have a graceful silent chorus.

- Write sentences, poems, or stories to music.

- Repeat or sing nursery rhymes in unison.

- Show rhythm and movement in a finger painting.

- Tell a story or read a book with characters acting out the parts.

- Listen to music. Listen for the musical beat of 3/4 or 4/4 or other rhythms.

Good Morning to You[67]

Choose the good morning greeting you wish to use and sing a welcome to start the school day. Some suggested variations are given. You may make up others. Sing "good morning" to... :

GOOD MORNING TO YOU

1. Good - morn - ing to you, Good - morn - ing to you;
2. Good - morn - ing to you, Good - morn - ing to you;

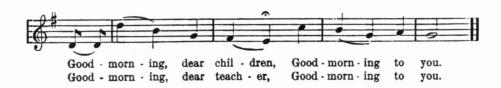

Good - morn - ing, dear chil - dren, Good - morn - ing to you.
Good - morn - ing, dear teach - er, Good - morn - ing to you.

Previous page: *"The Rhythm of Music" by Carol O'Regan.*

- Dear Children (Children nod in a recognition of each other as they sing).
- Dear Teacher.
- Dear _____ (Sing the name of a person having a birthday today.)
- Dear Principal ... Librarian ... Superintendent...

Happy Birthday to You!

To sing "Happy Birthday" use the same music for "Good Morning to You" and adapt for the birthday greeting. Many birthday songs have been written but this old favorite by Mildred & Patty Hill (1893) works best.

Musical Theater

The story, drama, and live action of theater are enjoyable. Many songs from musical theater are appropriate for young children. Consider your purposes and lesson objectives. Go to the public library and start your search in the 780s. Find some music you love and share with your children. Try 784.61[68] in your library. If you want to buy music cassettes, CDs, or sheet music for the piano or other instrument, visit the music store, music department of bookstores, or a specialty store. Buy music for your school or personal collections. My sources: I've heard some of these songs in the theater; I found some of the music in my local public library; and I own some of the musical scores. The songs and their sources are listed to help you locate the music and the words. I love these songs and recommend each one:

1. From *South Pacific*:

- "Dites-Moi: Tell Me Why?"[69] Children universally ask questions. Learn this lovely song and teach your children. Discuss the words and meaning.
- "Happy Talk."[70] Positive happy talk is the mood of this song. Motions include holding both hands as if they were mouths opening and closing, talking to each other, speaking "Happy Talk." After learning this song the motions can become a "hand-signal" for happy talk. See page 57.

2. From *The King and I*:

- "The March of Siamese Children."[71] Introduced by the King of Siam, the teacher, Mrs. Anna, meets the children. Find a CD of this grand march. Children would enjoy hearing and marching to this music.
- "Getting to Know You."[72] This is a fine song to teach children of all ages. In Shanghai, a group of Chinese Senior-Ladies sang this song in English and danced to the music for my American Touring Chorale group.[73] You could use this song for a parents program at the beginning of the school year.
- "I Whistle a Happy Tune."[74] For preschoolers who cannot yet whistle or just for fun, read Ezra Jack Keats' delightful book *Whistle for Willie*. Teach this lively song for fun. Also, as the song teaches, encourage children to sing whenever they're afraid.

3. From *Oklahoma!*:

- "Oh, What a Beautiful Morning"[75] is a refreshing positive song for any day. Sing or play the entire song for the children to hear. Teach the first part of the song. Children will enjoy seeing the movie version of the musical on a video, set at the place where "Curley" sings about the beautiful day. Before playing the tape, ask children to listen for the rhyme of "day" and "way." Depending on the ages of the children, you may want to write the words on the board and draw a simple sunshine.

- "Oklahoma."[76] Spelling the name of the state one letter at the time is fun in this sweeping song. O-k-l-a-h-o-m-a! Show children the location of the state on a map of the United States.

4. From *Carousel*:

- "June Is Bustin' Out All Over."[77] The energetic song could be used for fun near the end of school in the classroom. Or the music teacher may want to work with teachers in planning an end-of-school program using the song with motions, mime, or scenes showing some of the activities that children and faculty look forward to during the summer vacation. Because of the intricate rhythms of this song you may want to request several months ahead so the music teacher will have time to help children learn the song.

The youngest preschooler could learn to chant the underlying rhythm of "June, June, June, June," for others to sing over, "June Is Bustin' Out All Over."

- "You'll Never Walk Alone."[78] This moving song from *Carousel* is more like a hymn. Some of your children will have already experienced the dark storms of life and could use a clear dose of hope. Sing or play the song for the children. Some might like to learn to hum or sing phrases of the song.

The message of the song is that life can be faced with courage and hope, not fear and despair. Much symbolism will not be understood by some of the younger children. The song starts with a storm. All children know that a dark severe storm can be frightening. Mature children can listen for the signs of hope at the end of the song, a "golden sky"[79] and the "sweet, silver song"[80] of a bird. Strength is promised for the journey of life for "You'll Never Walk Alone" because God is walking with you.

Classical Musicians

Space does not allow for all the classical composers to be included here. Please try listening to some of the music. Introduce selections to your students. Play some of your favorites for your students, telling them why you like the composer or the music. Enjoy the music of the classical composers at various times in your school week.

Johann Sebastian Bach (1685–1750)

The Bachs were a family of musicians and Johann was a hard worker,

Johann Sebastian Bach.

producing more works than any other composer. German composer Johann Sebastian Bach was one of the geniuses of music.[81]

Ludwig Van Beethoven (1770–1827)

The German composer Beethoven is one of the giants of music. Today visitors can visit a museum at his birthplace in Bonn, Germany. Beethoven made his concert debut when he was only eight years old.

At age 31, Beethoven noticed he was growing deaf. He wrote beautiful music when he was totally deaf. Milton Cross wrote, "Deaf to the sounds of music, [Beethoven] sought to put down the turbulent and majestic sounds he heard within."[82]

Beethoven is mentioned in this book several times. Listen to the grandeur of his music. Find favorite pieces of music by Beethoven. The "Moonlight Sonata for the Piano" in C-sharp minor (Op. 27, No. 2) is a famous piano sonata.

BEETHOVEN'S FIFTH SYMPHONY

Sylvia Ashton-Warner, the extraordinary teacher from New Zealand, used the first eight notes of Beethoven's Fifth Symphony to get the attention of children. She played the piano and trained her students to stop whatever they were doing and look at her.[83] She used Beethoven's music as I used my signal, "Freeze!" (See page 57.) It occurs to me you could also sing this signal with syllables. Do you play another instrument? If you do not have a piano in your class, use a smaller instrument to play Beethoven's dramatic notes. Here is the memorable music:

"Beethoven's Fifth Symphony."

Johannes Brahms (1833–1897)

The German musician Johannes Brahms made up little melodies as a child. He was given piano lessons when he was ten and at fourteen gave a piano recital, "including one of his own pieces."[84]

JOHANNES BRAHMS LULLABY

The beautiful "Cradle Song" is also known as "Brahms Lullaby" and "Lullaby and Good Night." The master composer wrote peaceful soothing music in this lullaby. One version with music is given below. Because "The Cradle Song" is in the public domain there are many versions. Choose the words you prefer. I learned these from childhood:

"Harp sticker."

"Lullaby and good night, With roses delight.

With lilies over-head is baby's sweet bed.

Lay me down now and rest, may your slumber be blest,

Lay me down now and rest, may your slumber be blest."

— Brahms Lullaby

Suggestions: (1) Teachers may want to softly sing this gentle lullaby to begin nap time for preschoolers. (2) Make a tape recording of you, a faculty member, or another friend playing this piece on piano, harp, or violin. The instrumental without words is restful. (3) Buy a cassette tape or compact disc of a orchestration of some of Brahms' music. Play

Cradle Song

JOHANNES BRAHMS

"Brahms Lullabye."

the music for enjoyment; use as background music for naptime; "settling down music" after an active recess period; for relaxation on a rainy day when no outside exercise is possible; or for an art experience, "Paint to Music."

Claude Debussy (1862–1918)

Debussy's piano music includes a work he wrote for his daughter, "Chouchou." Milton Cross explains the suite "Children's Corner": Written between 1906 and 1908, English titles were used for the games played by an English governess for a French child.[85]

Six sections are in the piano music "Children's Corner":

1. Doctor. A child struggles with piano exercises.

2. Jimbo's Lullaby (A toy elephant).

3. Serenade of the Doll.

4. The Snow Is Dancing.

5. The Little Shepherd.

6. Golliwogg's Cake Walk.

The French composer Debussy wrote lovely music. Play some of his work about nature in honor of his August 22 birthday. Or play during your school day any time of the year. I think children would particularly enjoy these selections:

- "La Mer" means "The Sea." Ask children if they can hear in the music the sounds of waves crashing into the seashore.

- "Clair de Lune" means "Moonlight." Lovely soft sounds.

ACTIVITIES TO MUSIC:

1. Plan for children to paint or draw with one of these two works by Debussy playing softly in the background.

2. Dance to the music.

3. Play softly during naptime.

"LA MER"

Debussy, strongly attracted to the sea in boyhood, became a musician, but returned to his youthful dreams when he composed his great work, "La Mer" ("The Sea").

Check on the experiences of your classes. Ask children:

- Have you walked on the beach?

- Have you been swimming in the surf?

- Have you felt the splash of an ocean wave?

- Have you tasted salty sea water?

Debussy captured in sound the many moods, scenes, and feelings of the sea in his composition "La Mer." Play this music for your children.

THREE MOVEMENTS OF LA MER

The titles of the three movements are:

1. From dawn till noon on the sea.

2. Play of the waves.

3. Dialogue of the wind and the sea.

Edward Elgar (1857–1934)

Have you marched to the world famous music "Pomp and Circumstance"? If so you have heard the work of the English composer Sir Edward Elgar. I have marched to the majestic music on three occasions: graduation from high school, college, and graduate school. Buy a CD of "Pomp and Circumstance," March No. 2 in A minor, and play it for the children. If it was played at your graduation, tell them the story.

"Pomp and Circumstance" was actually the name of a set of five marches. But the second has become the famous work and is the one I recommend that you play for children. The origin of the phrase is actually from Shakespeare's *Othello*: "Pomp and circumstance of glorious war."[86]

Because you are an important influence on young children, I like to mention the childhood of the musicians included in this book. English composer Sir Edward Elgar grew up in an atmosphere of the arts. His father was an excellent musician, owned a music store, played violin in orchestras, and was organist at the Worcester Cathedral.[87]

Adults will also appreciate Elgar's beautiful and moving orchestral music "Variations on an Original Theme" (The Enigma Variations). You decide whether or not to play for your students.

George Gershwin (1898–1937)

A truly American composer, George Gershwin was born in Brooklyn and died in Hollywood. Gershwin was gifted with "inventiveness, fresh ideas, and a basic feeling for rhythm."[88] He had an influence on music in America.

From his major works, I believe children will enjoy parts of these selections:

- "An American in Paris." See suggestions on page 30.

- "Rhapsody in Blue." Tell children the title and let them paint with the color blue as you play this selection.

- Variations on "I Got rhythm," for piano.

Ferde Grofé
(1892–1972)

The best known work of Grofé (pronounced "groh FAY") is the *Grand Canyon Suite* (1931). I believe children will especially enjoy the third section, "On the Trail."

The American composer and arranger Grofé was born in New York City. For 14 years he arranged music for Paul Whiteman's band. Whiteman commissioned Grofé to do an arrangement for the band of Gershwin's "Rhapsody in Blue" (1924).

An odd piece was Grofé's "Symphony in Steel" (1937). The composer experimented with nonmusical sounds. Someone may have occasion to look for the music to listen for the sounds of a locomotive bell and a pneumatic drill.[89]

Joseph Haydn (1732–1809)

One of Austria's most celebrated musicians, Haydn responded even as an infant to the music around him. He sang the tunes he heard. At family concerts he picked up two sticks and pretended they were a violin and a bow! His professional training

"Violin sticker."

began when he was only six years of age.[90]

Wolfgang Amadeus Mozart
(1756–1791)

Musical genius is the correct term for Wolfgang Amadeus Mozart. His musical achievements in childhood were spectacular. Raised in a musical home, his father was a composer and violinist. There are amazing documented stories about young Mozart.[91]

Age 3. Mozart was interested in the harpsichord.

Age 4. His father gave him harpsichord lessons.

Age 5. Mozart tried to write music.

Age 6. Family tour. His father decided to show off Mozart. They visited in courts all over Europe.

Age 7. Mozart wrote a sonata.

Age 8. Mozart wrote a symphony.

Wolfgang Amadeus Mozart was born in Salzburg, Austria, and died in Vienna. He produced tremendous music for the world and died a pauper. Mozart's music had an "extraordinarily wide range." He was "a composer of many and varied moods."[92] He even did an improvisation on "The ABC Song." Mozart loved music, dancing, people, and life ... but always music.

Today expectant mothers listen to Mozart and soothe restless babies with his music. Be sure to play Mozart for your students. Listen to some of his music and choose your favorites.

Serge Prokofiev (1891–1953)

Russian musician Serge Prokofiev was born in the Ukraine and died in Moscow. Read about his childhood on page 88. At age 13 Prokofiev entered the St. Petersburg Conservatory where he studied for ten years. One of his teachers was Rimsky-Korsakov. In his lifetime Prokofiev was in, then out and then in again with Soviet officials. Milton Cross wrote about one such period in Prokofiev's life: "Prokofiev was becoming increasingly impatient with the new regime in Russia and the restrictions it placed on the free creative spirit."[93] He took an American tour playing in New York and Chicago. He made his home in Paris, taking concert tours in Europe and the United States for a while before returning home to Russia.

Read the delightful story about Prokofiev's childhood art work on page 88. Do you know the wonderful classical children's work *Peter and the Wolf*? Read the next few pages.

PETER AND THE WOLF

The Music:

Are you familiar with the musical fairy tale "Peter and the Wolf"? The delightful musical story introduces the instruments of an orchestra. The Russian composer Serge Prokofiev wrote the "symphonic fairy tale."[94] His purpose was to illustrate for children the instruments of the orchestra." The characters in the story are represented by instruments! At the beginning of the work the composer explains each character as he names their instrument via a narrator. "Prokofiev also assigns a specific descriptive little motif to each character."[95] When the child hears the repeated musical element that identifies the character, they know the action of the story by the music. Each musical element is called a motif.

The Musical Tale:

> Young children can grasp
> The uncomplicated story:

A young boy named Peter has been warned by his grandfather not to go into the meadow where a wolf lives. But the boy goes, encounters and captures the wolf, and triumphantly takes it to the zoo!

The Characters:

A flute is a bird.
An oboe is the duck.
A clarinet (playing in the low register)
    is the cat.

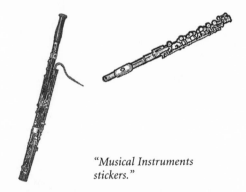

"Musical Instruments stickers."

A bassoon isthe grandfather.
Three horns signal the wolf.
A string quartet is Peter.
Timpani (kettledrums) and bass drums
    are the hunters shooting.

CHILDREN, MUSIC AND MUSICIANS

The Russian musician Prokofiev had written the words and music of two operas by age twelve.[96] His childhood was filled with music, for his mother was an excellent pianist and often played for him. Prokofiev described his early musical experiences in an autobiographical article: "My efforts consisted of either sitting at the piano and making up tunes which I could not write down, or sitting at the table and drawing notes which could not be played."[97]

Teachers, throughout the school year, encourage children to draw. When appropriate, tell this delightful story. Use first person:

"I Draw Circles" by the author.

I am a Russian boy. My name is Serge Prokofiev [SIR' j-pro KO fe f]. I like to draw circles. I like hearing music too. My mother plays the piano all the time. She is wonderful. I really love music. When I play with other children or see them at school, they draw trains and people, flowers, and buildings. I just draw music notes! I like to draw music notes. I draw music notes like designs. Every day I see notes on the piano stand. I love music. What do you like?

Notes on Prokofiev: Read more about Prokofiev on page 87. See also: *Peter and the Wolf*, page 87. Tell the first person story of the Russian boy, Prokofiev. Make a silhouette of a music note and show the note to the children when you tell them the story about Prokofiev's drawings. See page 77.

Maurice Ravel (1875–1937)

"You must tell the children about *Bolero*," my husband insisted this morning. Children may have heard this music on cartoons or at ice skating productions.

Maurice Ravel, born in Ciboure and died in Paris, was a French musician. In his later life he recalled his love of music: "From my early childhood I was interested in music."[98] As a child Ravel played piano duets with his father. A strong Spanish influence is heard in Ravel's music. "Born on the border of Spain, he continued to be fascinated all his life with Spanish music, dance, and geography."[99]

Frenchman Ravel did an extended concert tour of the United States early in 1928. The same year the dancer Ida Rubinstein commissioned him to write a work for her. The ballet *Bolero* was his greatest musical success.[100] First performed in Paris in November 1928, it was first performed in the United States on November 14, 1929, conducted by Toscanini. The strong, rhythmic music has long repetitions and builds to a dramatic climax, then abruptly stops. "The entire piece is 17 minutes. A side drum punctuates the bolero rhythm."[101] The still popular music is played at symphony programs and band concerts and has been adapted by jazz bands and many different instruments.[102] Try Ravel's *Bolero* with your children.

Nicholas Rimsky-Korsakov
(1844–1908)

THE COMPOSER

Russian musician Nicholas Andreievitch Rimsky-Korsakov was

"Drum Sticker."

born in Tikhvin (Norgorod district) on March 18, 1844, and died in St. Petersburg on June 21, 1908. In reading about Rimsky-Korsakov, I see the rhythm of two passions of his life: music and the sea.

1. Music. He responded to music in his childhood home. We have his words of those early years. Some of the quotes are given for your information and encouragement. From the autobiography of Nicholas Rimsky-Korsakov.[103]

Age 2: "I was not fully two years old when I clearly distinguished all the tunes my mother sang to me."

Age 3 or 4: "I beat a toy drum in perfect time, while my father played the piano. My father would change the tempo and rhythm on purpose, and I followed suit at once."

Age 5: "I began to sing quite correctly, whatever my father played. Often I sang along with him."

Age 6: "On the piano, I picked out the pieces and accompaniments I heard my father perform. I learned the names of the notes and could recognize and name any note of the piano."

Age 8: Studied piano with local teachers.

Age 9: Began composing.

2. The Sea. Remember there were two passions in the life of Nicholas Rimsky-Korsakoff. As a child "he read books about the sea; built model ships; memorized and quoted nautical terms."[104] Family members had Navy careers and he attended the Naval Academy (1862–1865) where a graduation

requirement was a world cruise. He set sail on the *Almaz* in April 1862 and even visited the United States before returning as a naval officer to Russia. In St. Petersburg he began to study music again.

MUSICAL RECORDINGS

Introduce children to the musical fairy tale *Scheherazade* (July 1888), a symphonic suite written after the Oriental *Arabian Nights*. I've enjoyed this work from a young age. Looking at the album cover of my "antique recordings" today evokes sounds of the music in my mind.

THEMES OF SCHEHERAZADE[105]

Two major themes mold the four movements of the suite together:

(1) The theme of the strong sultan.

(2) The sound of Scheherazade represented by "a tender violin solo, in triplets."

Sometimes a minor theme is heard representing Sinbad the Sailor's ship, "first in solo flute, then in oboe and the clarinet."

THE MUSIC

Scheherazade, Opus 35, includes these complete movements:

1. "The Sea and Sinbad's Ship." The Sultan theme begins this episode "in unison brass with woodwinds and strings."

2. "The Tale of Prince Kalender." The Scheherazade theme introduces this movement.

3. "The Young Prince and the Princess" is a love song. Children might enjoy listening in this movement for the "rhythmic background by triangle, tambourine, cymbals, and snare drum."

4. "The Festival at Bagdad; the Sea; the Ship Founders on the Rocks." There are dramatic changes in the final movement, concluding with Scheherazade finishing her tales and winning over the Sultan.

THE SEA AGAIN

You noticed the importance of the love of the sea in these musical themes of Rimsky-Korsakov. Being at sea on his world cruise after naval school influenced him profoundly. He thought he'd given up music during this time but certainly was intrinsically experiencing the rhythm and music of the sea. His two passions — music and the sea — came together in his life.

PLAY THE MUSIC OF SCHEHERAZADE

Obtain a CD or cassette tape and listen to some of the music yourself. Put the music on to play at home while you do chores and notice which pieces catch your attention. Decide which ones to play for the children.

Or you may decide to play the entire work for children depending on your own love for the music; the intended use of the music; your purposes; and the musical experiences of your students. This could well become one of the students' favorite classical works. Become acquainted with *Scheherazade*.

BIOGRAPHY

Enjoy learning fascinating facts and stories about people. You can see by these short biographical sketches how the life, interests, and experiences of Rimsky-Korsakov and other musicians influenced the people and their music. Go to your library and learn more about other musicians, authors, poets, and artists. Share interesting data from their lives to help children connect with their own interests.

Camille Saint-Saëns (1835–1921)[106]

Saint-Saëns is considered one of the great musicians of France. Listen to his music from *The Carnival of Animals* and choose selections for your children to hear.

Peter Ilitch Tchaikovsky

(1840–1893)

The great Russian composer Tchaikovsky had a sad and troubled life. He first studied law, not music. Finally in 1861 he seriously considered music as a career because it was the only thing that interested him. He had become lazy but changed and worked hard *inspired by his teacher*.[107] Many have called him the greatest of Russian composers.

Children have heard some of Tchaikovsky's music in the background of movie scores, on cartoons, on television specials, and even television commercials. The year that music from Tchaikovsky's *The Nutcracker* ballet was on a cat-food commercial helped me decide to plan a series of lessons for children in my school library. Teachers and children enthusiastically received the lessons and the wonderful music. Decide to share with the children you care about some of the classical music in this chapter.

"THE 1812 OVERTURE"

- "The 1812 Overture" was commissioned for a dedication of a church in Moscow, built because Napoleon was defeated in Russia in 1812. Tchaikovsky planned the music to be played outside and wrote "a thunderous climax"[108] into the scoring for the percussion section. Play a recording of the end of "The 1812 Overture" for your children. Have them listen for the dramatic ending with real cannons firing.

The annual "Boston Pops Fourth of July Concert" concludes with this great music by Tchaikovsky including the cannons! Tell children to watch for the program on television this summer.

"Cymbals Sticker."

THE NUTCRACKER

- *The Nutcracker* (or Casse-Noisette) by Tchaikovsky was first a story by E. T. A. Hoffmann adapted by Dumas.[109] At Christmastime a little girl receives a toy nutcracker and dreams it is a handsome prince who takes her on a dream trip. Children will especially enjoy these selections:

- "The Miniature Overture." An introduction to the work.

- "Dance of the Sugarplum Fairy."
- "Trepak." Boys too enjoy this Russian dance with a fast rhythm.
- "Arab Dance" features a clarinet.
- A "Chinese Dance" lets the children hear the flute and the piccolo.
- The "Waltz of the Flowers" is especially lovely.

7

Rhythms, Poems, and Poets

Rhythms

Sea Sounds

> Listen to the motion
> Of the ocean
> As the waves
> Lap the shore.
>
> — G.M. Caughman

Rhythm is delightful. To share and experience rhythm with children is a double delight. Try reading or saying the above words aloud to children. Say each word distinctly. Remember to read this when you have pictures or stories about the sea or the ocean.

Help for Teacher: If you have trouble hearing or feeling the rhythm of "Sea Sounds" above, try this alone. Notice the rhythm of four counts in each line:

> Lis'-ten' to' the' (1, 2, 3, 4)
> Mo'-tion' of' the' (1, 2, 3, 4)
> O'-cean' as' the' (1, 2, 3, 4)
> Waves' lap' the' shore' (1, 2, 3, 4)

Then clap the rhythm softly to yourself as you read above. Next go back to "Sea Sounds" and read in a rhythm. Repeat but don't do the 1, 2, 3, 4, like a drill, let the words flow. Do you hear the rhythm? Do you feel the rhythm? Now go enjoy the rhythm of words with children!

A true story: My nice niece[110] and I sat on the front porch of her country home. The rain prevented the walk in the yard we'd planned. This verse popped into my mind as I watched the rhythm of the rain. We shared a lovely afternoon watching the rain and experimenting

with the rhythm of the rhyme. Memorize and be ready to enjoy the rhythm of the rhyme in a lovely rain!

Rain[111]

Rain- - -,
Rain- - -,
Rain on green grass,
Rain on the tree;
Rain on the rooftop;
But not on me.
Rain- - -,
Rain- - -.

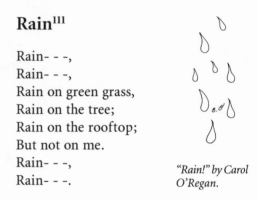

"Rain!" by Carol O'Regan.

Motions: [Clap to make rhythm as spaces indicate. Clap at beginning and end.] [Flutter fingers up and down.] [Raise both hands to form a tree.] [Use hands above head to make roof, palms down, fingertips touching.] [Clap softly and fade as though rain is stopping.]

Let's go on a bear hunt![3]

Directions: "The Bear Hunt" is such fun. I enjoyed this active game as a child. Learn this game, practice with the motions, and enjoy with all ages! You will be the leader. Others will be instructed to follow the leader, repeating your words and motions. An alternate way to begin the game is to privately enlist an assistant who will be asked to help you begin. You and your helper will

---

Previous Page: *"Poetry Gives Our Spirit Wings" (courtesy Library of Congress, Center for the Book).*

begin saying and repeating the words and motions. Others will quickly "catch on" and join you on the "Bear Hunt." Enjoy!

The Bear Hunt

Let's go on a bear hunt.
All right.
Let's go.
Oh, look,
I see a wheat field!
Can't go around it,
Can't go under it,
Let's go through it.
All right.
Let's go.
Swish, swish, swish.

Oh look,
I see a tree!
Can't go over it,
Let's climb up.
All right.
Let's go.

Oh look,
I see a swamp!
Can't go around it.
Can't go under it.
Let's swim through it.
All right.
Let's go.

Oh look,
I see a bridge!
Can't go around it,
Can't go under it.
Let's cross over it
All right,
Let's go.

Oh look,
I see a cave!

Can't go around it,
Can't go under it.
Let's go in it.
All right.
Let's go.

My, my, it's dark in here.
Better use my flashlight.
Doesn't work.
I think I see something.
It's big!
It's furry!
It has a big nose!
I think — it's a bear!
It is a Bear!
Let's Go!

[Repeat everything backwards. Sound rushed and anxious. At the end, pretend to wipe brow. Give a loud sigh of relief.]

Actions: Start slow. Tap hands on thighs like walking. Rub hands together. Sounds like swishing wheat. Pretend to climb tree. At the top, place hand on forehead. Look around. Climb down. Pretend to swim. Stamp feet and make a clicking sound with tongue. Cup hands to make hollow sound when clapping. Speak with suspense in voice.

Get out of the cave.

Cross over the bridge.

Swim through the swamp.

Climb up the tree.

Climb down the tree.

Go through the wheat field.

We're Home!

Whew! We made it!

Repeat motions of each. Pause between places. Wipe brow. Look relieved.

Teddy Bear

This rhythm can be used for a school-wide Bear Day; for a "Teddy Bear's Picnic" or outside in springtime as a jump rope rhyme. Children enjoy the rhythm.

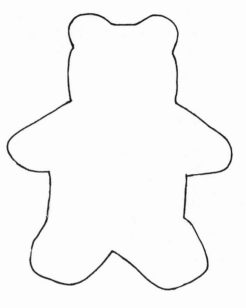

"Teddy Bear Name tag" by the author.

Teddy bear, teddy bear,

Turn around;

Teddy bear, teddy bear,

Touch the ground.

Teddy bear, teddy bear,

Show your shoe;

Teddy bear, teddy bear, that will do.

Teddy bear, teddy bear,

Go upstairs;

Teddy bear, teddy bear,

Say your prayers;

Teddy bear, teddy bear,

Turn out the light;

Teddy bear, teddy bear,

Say, "Good-night!"[112]

Poetry

I'm Glad

I'm glad the sky is painted blue,
The earth is painted green,
With such a lot of nice fresh air
All sandwiched in between.

— Anonymous

Spring Songs

Spring morning sounds:
Doves coo,
Cardinals chirp,
Robins sing.
Mocking birds
Warble them all.
Spring Songs.

— G.M. Caughman

Courtesy Library of Congress, Center for the Book.

In the South

Not unusual to us,

We eat dinner at noon,

We eat supper at night.

In the South, in the South.

There is chicken fried steak,

White gravy on the side.

Butter beans and mayonnaise.

In the South, in the South.

Vine ripened sliced tomatoes,

Cornbread and turnip greens.

Lots of sweet lemon tea,

In the South, in the South.

Sitting on the porch swing,

Watching lightning bugs glow

A contented feeling.

In the South, in the South.

Y'all Come!!!

— G. M. Caughman

A Great Gray Elephant

A great gray elephant,

A little yellow bee,

A tiny purple violet,

A tall green tree,

A red and white sailboat

On a blue sea —

All these things

You gave to me,

When you made

My eyes to see —

Thank you, God.

— courtesy The National Society for
the Prevention of Blindness

Breakfast[113]

The spoon cuts small rounds

Up to the mouth, and

The teeth bite down

Into the soft,

Pale orange fruit.

What a funny name!

The fruit with seeds hollowed —

Sounds like a game

Or an animal.

Cantaloupe!

— G.M. Caughman

Funny Poems

In *Chicken Socks* Brod Bagert[114] the New Orleans lawyer turned poet has several funny poems to read aloud to young children. I like these:

SILLY:

- "The Bad Mood Bug," page 16. Read to make preschoolers and first graders laugh when someone is grouchy.

- "Chicken Socks," page 7. Ask: "Can you laugh when you're sick?" Most children like to wear large fuzzy slippers and will laugh at the chickens and the slippers by Tim Ellis.

- "The Easter Kitchen," page 26, about a messy job of dying eggs.

CHILD EXPERIENCE:

- "The Time I Learned to Ride My Bike," pages 18–19. All young children will identify with this poem either because they desire to or have learned to ride a bike.

Poets

Christina Rosseti (1830–1894)

Christina Rossetti lived in London where her father, a distinguished Italian scholar, met his wife Frances Polidori, and raised his family. The four children — Maria Francesca, William Michael, Dante Gabriel, and Christina Georgina — were intellectually stimulated by her father's Italian family and friends, musicians, writers, and artists. Teachers interested in literature and art will be interested in her life. The poet and painter Dante Gabriel Rossetti was Christina's brother. She was the model for several pre–Raphaelite paintings. Author May Hill Arbuthnot groups Shakespeare, Blake and Rossetti as "Singers of Songs."[115] Christina wrote a lovely group of verses titled *Sing Song* in 1872. She became an invalid and died at age 64. She was in pain yet wrote these happy verses and translated them into Italian, *Ninna Nanna*.[116]

Two of her delightful verses are included in this book: the color poem "What Is Pink," page 108, and "The Wind."

The Wind

Who has seen the wind?
Neither I nor you:
But when the leaves hang trembling
The wind is passing thro'.

Who has seen the wind?
Neither you nor I:
But when the trees bow down their
  heads
The wind is passing by.

— Christina Rossetti
Sing Song, 1872

Robert Louis Stevenson

(1850–1894)

Scottish author Robert Louis Balfour Stevenson became famous worldwide and with all ages. Introduce young children to his classic of children's literature *A Child's Garden of Verses* (1885), and later in life they can read the exciting adventure stories *Treasure Island* (1883) and *Kidnapped* (1886). Stevenson's interests are evident in his poems and stories. He loved the sea, adventure, and reading books. He especially enjoyed reading literature and history. He traveled widely even though he was in frail health. Read all about his fascinating life in your school or public library. Stevenson's tombstone has lines from his poem "Requiem."

"Here he lies where he longed to be;
Home is the sailor, home from the sea,
And the hunter, home from the hill.[117]"

For a while it was hard to find a copy of *A Child's Garden of Verses*, the classic children's poems by Robert Louis Stevenson. Now there are again several editions on the market. Go to a bookstore, ask to see several, and choose your favorite edition. You'll probably want to own a copy of this work. I own four. I still have two editions of my childhood poems, *A Child's Garden of Verses*. I loved these verses and still do. My mother read them to me, I read them to my children Cathy and Bill, I read them to my classes in public school, and look forward to reading them to my grandchildren. Memorize some of the verses so you can quote them in appropriate places such as on the beach and in the rain. Don't miss these classic verses. Are your choices included in my list of favorites?

- The Swing
- Singing
- The Land of Counterpane
- Rain
- At the Seaside
- Foreign Lands
- Time to Rise
- The Cow
- My Shadow
- The Land of Storybooks

"The Swing" by Joey Weber.

- The Lamplighter

- My Bed Is a Boat

- Bed in Summer

- Marching Song

Rain

The rain is raining all around
It falls on field and tree,
It rains on the umbrellas here,
And on the ships at sea.

— Robert Louis Stevenson, 1885,
from *A Child's Garden of Verses*

"Rain" by the author.

More Poetry

Honey, I Love is by Eloise Greenfield, with pictures by Diane and Leo Dillon. Rush and buy your personal copy of this lovely book. The partnership of author and illustrators is a perfect marriage. This book of love and joy is both delightful to hold (it's a small book, 7½ × 5¼) and delightful to read. Read silently, then share with a friend or a class. The striking illustrations add to the charm of the book. Child-like brown block prints are charming while the soft black charcoal drawings are exquisite. I have bought both the hardcover and paperback editions, personally and processed library editions for school libraries. The publisher has printed "Ages 5–8" on the book blurb but I recommend the book for *all* ages. Use the following suggestions. After you read the book, you'll think of more. Honey, I love this book!

- The title poem is a beautiful look at a loving family in the Southern United States. Reading this poem inspired me to write a fun poem about the South. (See page 97.)

- A sweet and sad poem, "Keepsake" allows a poignant look into a child's feelings after the death of a friend.

- Read Eloise Greenfield's poem "Lessie" for a perfect introduction to Katherine Paterson's Newbery winner, *Bridge to Terabithia*. I wrote a booktalk to introduce fourth, fifth, and sixth graders to Paterson's book. Though the Newbery winner is too advanced for preschoolers and younger children in the focus of the present book, I list it here to illustrate my belief that all ages can enjoy Greenfield's poetry of the heart.

- "I Look Pretty" is a fun read for preschoolers about dressing up. I have a "play clothes box" for young children. A fun activity is to let some children "dress up," then model their "outfits" while you re-read the poem to the class. Some children may want to take real or pretend pictures with a camera as seen in the block-prints.

- Enjoy the rhythm and music of "Way Down in the Music." Children ask for these poems to be read more than once. Before sharing with children, practice reading this poem aloud at home until you can feel the music.

- The delightful poem "Fun" reminds me of three teachers of mine who played piano. I can imagine Mrs. Key, Mrs. Bell or Miss Ward in this situation. (My teachers in first grade, seventh grade, and college kindergarten education classes!)

- Children enjoy "Rope Rhythm" the first and twenty-first time they hear it read. Read and wait for the sounds: "Read it again, teacher."

- Three times I have heard Ashley Bryan delight adult audiences with an interactive performance of Eloise Greenfield's "Things." The surprise ending focuses on something that lasts longer than material things: a poem!

- Read "Harriet Tubman" during Black History Month.

- Developing a child's self-worth is a goal of every caring teacher. The poem "By Myself" is a playful look at the self.

- A number of books have been printed to help pre-school and young children deal with the fact of a baby brother or sister in their life. "Moochie" is a playful poem that helps the child feel much older and more accepting of a baby in the family.

- Many poems can be enjoyed by leading children into the poem with questions that help them relate to the topic. Read a poem from Eloise Greenfield's book or choose another poem you like and write your questions. An example follows related to the subject "Trains."

- Trains. Ask the question: "Have you ever ridden on a train? (Discuss.)

  Then introduce the poem from the book *Honey I Love* by asking a question: "Is this how riding on a train feels?" Read aloud: "Riding on the Train." Then ask: "What's happening during the poem?" (Sights are passing quickly.) Ask: "What happened at the end of the poem?" (She went to sleep.) Read poem again for enjoyment.

Relate poems to social studies:
From *Chicken Socks:*

- "Progress," page 17. Regarding technology.

- "Paleontology," page 21. Activity: Introduce children to paleontology. Hide seashells and "fossils" in a sand-filled dry swimming pool. Give each child an "exploring kit" (a brown paper bag filled with a clean paint brush and a plastic spoon). Let children search for "treasures." For fun read this poem.

Chicken Socks: And Other Conta-gious Poems. By Brod Bagert. Illustra-tions by Tim Ellis. WordSong (Boyds Mills Press, Inc.: A Highlights Com-pany). LC# 93-604749[118]

April Bubbles Chocolate

Lee Bennett Hopkins is an admirable compiler of poetry. *April Bubbles Choco-late* is subtitled *An ABC of Poetry* (Simon & Schuster, 1994). Not a true alphabet book, its unifying theme is that each poem begins with or features a letter of the alphabet. I particularly like several poems I hadn't seen before. They would be excellent to use one at a time. Enjoy the illustrations by Barry Root and read these poems aloud with your stu-dents:

- Carl Sandburg did a poem titled "Bubbles," with rainbows.

- Read "Kitten."

- "Now" is to read when school begins.

- Librarian, be sure to read "Quiet" by the excellent poet Myra Cohn Livingston the first time you have library class; or, teacher, before your class goes to the school library.

- David McCord's "Yellow" is sur-prising and delicious.

- This anthology contains a familiar but favorite poem of mine, "Dreams" by Langston Hughes.

The poetry collection *Night on Neighborhood Street* by Eloise Greenfield is filled with passion, reality, rhythm and rhyme, love and hope.[119]

Artist Jan Spivey Gilchrist created the soft emotion-packed illustrations for *Night on Neighborhood Street.* The gouache paintings highlighted with pas-tels are a visual treat for children and teachers alike.

Hold open the large book (10¾" × 8¾") allowing children to enjoy the illus-trations as you read text. Try these teach-ing suggestions for using the book and the individual poems throughout the school year:

- Always read poems to children first of all for enjoyment.

- Enjoy the book as a whole. Use like this: Introduce book by first open-ing front and back cover, show chil-dren and read words on cover. (These words are the title, author, and illustrator.) Then pause and let children enjoy art in silence. Allow them to comment. After a few moments, if they say nothing, stim-ulate thought and discussion by asking questions such as: "What is happening in the picture?" "What is the boy doing?" "Do you think he is dreaming? Does the name of the book, the title, give you any clues what the book might be about?" (FYI: Art shows a boy asleep in bed, his head resting on this pillow. The background shows a starry night, a river, an outline of a city with city lights and a large bright moon lighting the sky.) Then say: "Let's look inside the book and find out what's happening on Neighborhood Street."

- Read the first poem, "Neighborhood Street," for the enjoyment of rhythm and rhyme. Afterward ask the children to tell you the "story"

of the poem. Let several share "life stories" of their neighborhood, their street, their homes.

- Read *And to Think That I Saw It on Mulberry Street* by Dr. Seuss.

Writing Poetry

Many teachers enjoy reading short poems to children to begin class or at other times throughout the day. This book will aid you in giving children experiences with poetry and the rhythm of words. Read nursery rhymes aloud, play games with rhythms, and train the ear to enjoy poems that rhyme and also those in free verse.

From the time children learn to write, they can be guided to write from their experience and feelings. I believe learning to read and learning to write go together. A typical first- or second-grade sentence might be about the day, the weather, the child, and their family. The teacher can ask questions that will guide the child to include thoughts and feelings about facts and you have poetic writing.

Children learn: "A sentence is a group of words that make sense." You have taught them to write. Then a practical class assignment: "Write some sentences about yourself or about today." Thus a typical sentence might be:

My name is Kyle.
I am six years old.

or

Today is Monday.
I am at school.

Why not ask a few questions to guide children to think about their feelings and experiences. Give them the freedom to misspell words during "writing" or "poetry time" or whatever name you give this block of time in your week. Offer to spell words as needed. Start with questions and conversation such as: "What kind of day are we having? What do you hear? How do you feel today? What happened to you yesterday?" Ask children to listen to you until they get an idea, look down and begin writing. When everyone is writing you will stop talking to give them think time.

I remember a first grader's poetic writing:

The sky is blue. The sun is shining.
I hear Joseph cutting the green grass.

And another child's deep feelings:

Today I feel sad.
My puppy died.

"Poetry Time" Lesson Plan: One day in your week designate a space for poetry reading and writing. Decide on a name. "Poetry Time!" Instructions:

1. Have children clear their desks; then get out one piece of paper and a

pencil; get comfortable; listen, think, and enjoy writing.

2. Read a poem or several poems. Give suggestions for writing. Talk about the topic until children begin writing.

3. Stop. When all the children are writing or thinking about writing stop speaking. Insist on silence in the room.

4. Help individuals. Silently walk around and help. Spell words softly when asked, or even better: Write spellings the children need on the board.

5. Time. After a designated time of writing give a five minute warning when it's almost time to stop. Say, "You will need to try to get to a stopping place in five minutes."

6. Ask for volunteers to read their work aloud. "Who would like to share?" Writing is personal. Do not force anyone to read aloud. Be encouraging and supportive.

Many schools are now helping children express themselves in writing. Hearing Kenneth Koch speak inspired the author and many teachers to try some new ideas in poetry writing with children. Koch teaches reading and writing poetry as one subject. He uses "poetry ideas" which he calls "suggestions to the children for writing poems of their own."[120]

Try some ideas of Kenneth Koch:

- Suggest every line of a poem begin with "I wish."[121]

- Talk to an animal.[122]

- Write about something you think is beautiful that others do not.[123]

- Write a poem about something that you love to eat or drink.[124]

The title for one of Koch's books came from a poem by a child: *Rose, Where Did You Get That Red?* I have tried many of his ideas. If you need more help guiding children in poetry writing, look in your public library for these two books by Kenneth Koch:

- *Wishes, Lies, and Dreams: Teaching Children to Write Poetry*

- *Rose, Where Did You Get That Red? Teaching Great Poetry to Children.*

Dogs

Dogs are nice

Dogs are mean

Their sense of humor is very keen

They often chase after cats

And eat up ladies' pretty hats.

— Kim McKinney

Eagle

Eagles soar through the sky

Though they're very shy.

I talk to him and ask,

"Is flying a scary task?"

He answers me in a squawk,

"I would hate to ever walk."

— Mary Billiot

Cheetah

This one animal is very beautiful

It looks like shining brass

This one animal runs very fast.

— Tina Kirby

Nature Poems

These beautiful nature poems were written by a teacher.[125] Read to your children:

Flowers

Morning glory white
Trumpeting another day
Welcome early sight.

— Margaret Ann Cummings

Cobwebs

Lacy silver net
Draped between the milkweed stalks
Spiders home sweet home.

— Margaret Ann Cummings

How to begin writing a poem? Record your thoughts. Scribble words, reflections, and ideas in a teaching journal. Later take time to play with the words. Rearrange thoughts. Condense ideas into fewer words for an interesting exercise in discipline. The words do not have to rhyme. You may have a gift for rhyme. If you do, write that way. For me, free verse is such fun to write. You'll find several of my "poems" scattered throughout this text.

Take time to read rhymes, rhythms, verse, limericks, and poems. Visit the library and browse in the 800s section. Dip into several types of verse until you find favorite ones. Poems and verse can add meaning to your life. Read poetry for your enjoyment. Make notes of poems on 5 × 8 index cards of poems you want to remember, read again, or read to your classes. Buy poetry books.

Read poems to children! Read aloud. Read Mother Goose rhymes. Read poems with rhythm. Read poems that rhyme. Read poems that don't rhyme. Read silly poems. Read nonsense poems. Read happy poems. Read sad poems. Read thoughtful poems. Have fun sharing poetry.

Write Poetry about Children

Teacher, try to express in free verse some of your impressions about the children you teach. Keep the writing in a private place in your desk or briefcase. What to express? Anything! Your feelings and your observations. The actions, talent, or potential of the children. Play with the words. Simplify the thoughts into a few words. Sometimes it's harder to be concise than to use many words.

I'm working on an assignment now that has a very specific line count. At the same time I'm writing this book with many pages. Both are enjoyable as well as challenging.

A timeline of a personal example to encourage you to write poetry:

1. July 6, 1998. Scribbles of specific observations. I label: "Draft: Alexis" and

place in the Poetry folder in my top left desk drawer.[126]

2. October 1998. Alexis and I talk about art. I show her some personal art originals.

3. November 1998. Alexis sketches a snail for me that she saw in her mother's flower bed. She had made a sketch at home in her art journal.

4. February 12, 1999. Several months later I play with some of the words in my folder: "Poem Ideas." I rework the draft titled: "Alexis."

5. February 12, 1999. Decide I like the poem and want to finalize and give to the child's mother, as an encouragement. She's a single parent.

6. February 23, 1999. Decide to print part of poem in my book.

7. April 15, 1999. Ask the mother for permission. Here's only part of the poem I wrote for her mother.[127]

Alexis

Thoughtful,
Sensitive,
She wants to draw.

Daily she observes.
One night she notices
The full moon is not yellow:
White orb with gray.

Watching movement
In her Mother's garden
She runs for her journal
And sketches a snail.
Alexis

— G.M. Caughman

"My Snail" by Alexis.

8

Rhythm of Color and Art

Ribbons, Prisms, and Rainbows

I'll tell you how the sun rose —
A ribbon at a time.

         — Emily Dickinson, 1862

Color

When have you last seen a sunrise or a sunset? Each one is unique! How color does brighten and beautify our world! Help children have pleasurable experiences with color as they learn. Color is delightful. Enrich their lives and yours too with spots, dots,[128] and splashes of color. Place a single blossom on your desk or on a windowsill. Enjoy experiencing color. Look for ribbons with many colors. Place a set of pencil crayons in a mug on your desk. Plant a colorful bulb and anticipate the bloom. Read poems using color words. Hang a prism in a window. Take nature walks looking for a specific color. Study one color at a time for a week. Learn to sign color words. Use crayons[129] and paints generously in art and craft activities. Ask the children to tell or write true stories about seeing colors or rainbows.

Color Wheel

For a delightful introduction to the color wheel, read *Color Dance* by Ann Jonas. Hold the book so the children can easily see the waves of color move in the arms of the dancers. Read slowly to give the children time to enjoy the colors. Three dancers begin the color fantasy, four conclude. This book is a visual delight. Read for enjoyment.[130]

The children will begin to see the relationship between colors. For any child who is interested in colors or asks "why" or "how" type questions, be sure to read the explanations about the color wheel at the conclusion of the story. Some of the unusual color names and combinations are included: magenta, chartreuse, and vermilion are wonderful words and pleasant color names.

Primary color names: red, yellow, blue. Connect these three colors on the wheel to form a triangle pointing up.

Secondary color names: orange, green, purple. Connect these three colors on the wheel to form a triangle pointing down.

Color Poem: What Is Pink?[131]

What is pink?
A rose is pink.

What is yellow?
Pears are yellow,
Rich and ripe and mellow.

What is green?
The grass is green,
With small flowers between.

What is violet?
Clouds are violet
In the summer twilight.

What is orange?
Why an orange,
Just an orange!

         — Christina Rossetti (1830–1894)
                  Sing Song, 1872

"Rhythm" by Carol O'Regan.

Activities with Color

- Have a "Crayola" Dress-Up Day. Let children wear primary colors and secondary colors: red, yellow, blue, orange, green, violet.

- Read *Color Dance* (Jonas). Make a class "Color Wheel."

- Learn color words in sign language.

- Go on a nature walk. Ask: "How many shades of green can we find today?"

- Name other colors to look for on a nature walk.

- In Fall ask: "What are the colors of Autumn? Let's take a walk today. Look carefully and let's discover for ourselves!" Vary question for Spring.

- Bring a beautiful flower bud or blossom to school for your desk. Do you have these lovely flowers? roses — red, yellow, or pink; hibiscus — red or golden; colorful pansies; camellias — red or pink; purple iris; red geranium. Write the name of the flower and the color word on the chalkboard.

- Have a dramatic science lesson for the children showing the primary colors forming secondary colors. Preparation: Obtain 4 large jars. Mix powdered tempera paint with water and place in three jars, one each of red, yellow, and blue. Fill one jar with clear water to clean brushes. Use a paintbrush on a paper-covered easel and show the resulting secondary colors. It's fun to see the colors change before your eyes.

- Grow a pink or lavender African Violet in your room if you have a good light source.

- Plant a Spring bulb in December or January and watch for the sprouting and blooming. Science lesson: Measure growth weekly and make a graph.

- Make "Crayon Cups" in an old muffin tin[132] from broken Crayola *wax* crayons.

- Speak the rhythm of the Color Game: How Does Red Taste?"

- Read these books and observe if children notice the use of color and black-and-white. *The Seeing Stick* and *About Handicaps*. Stunning!

- Read *I See a Song* (Eric Carle). Let children use their imaginations to create a picture as you read. Supply: crayons, felt-tip markers, or paint.

- Read *The House of Four Seasons* by Roger Duvoisin.

- Read and enjoy Tomie de Paola's autobiographical book *The Art Lesson*.

- Rainbows. Notice rainbows after a rain. There has to be sunshine to make a rainbow. Go outside on the playground to view a rainbow if the danger of lightning is past. Provide felt-tip markers and large paper.

- Prism. Hang a prism in a window where the sun will shine through and create splashes of color. Note: Use clear fishing line.

- ROY G. BIV. To remember that red is on the top of a rainbow and to learn the other colors in order, memorize the funny name, Roy G. Biv. The colors in order from the top of a rainbow are Red, Orange, Yellow, Green, Blue, Indigo, and Violet.

- Enjoy the rhythm of reading poems or playing games with color words: A Great Gray Elephant, page 97; What Color: Who Is Wearing Red Today? page 111; I'm Glad, page 96; What Is Pink? page 108; Sing: A Color Review, page 77.

- Sing. Review the primary colors with a song using the melody "Mary Had a Little Lamb": "Who is wearing red today, red today, red today? Who is wearing red today? Please

hold up your hand." Repeat the song with other colors. Music page 62.

- Read a clever story of colors. All the animals have their own color — gray elephants, pink pigs — except for the chameleon. The chameleon has no color of his own. Leo Lionni solves a problem with a story. *A Color of His Own.*

- Read Shel Silverstein's humorous poem "Colors" from *Where the Sidewalk Ends* on page 24 in his book.

- On a commuter train from New York to Connecticut, artist Leo Lionni tore bits of paper from a magazine and made up a story to entertain his two grandchildren, and *Little Blue and Little Yellow* was created.

Color Words in Sign Language

Learn these color words in sign language and teach them to your children:

Red, see page 111. Blue, see page 113. Yellow, see page 112. Green, see page 114. Orange, see page 114. Purple, see page 115. Brown, see page 110. Black, see page 110. White, see page 111. All sign illustrations are courtesy of Gallaudet University, Washington, D.C.

black
negro

brown
moreno

Left: *Sign "black."* Above: *Sign "brown" (courtesy of Gallaudet University, Washington, D.C.).*

white
blanco

Sign "white" (courtesy of Gallaudet University, Washington, D.C.).

Red

- Red in French, *rouge*; Spanish, *rojo*.

- Game: Who is Wearing Red? See words, pages 111–112.

- Red Sailboat. Read the poem "A Great Gray Elephant" on page 97. Ask: "What is red?"

- Nature. Thinking About Nature. Ask children to think about outside and name anything in nature that is red. (Tomato; strawberry; cherry; red apple; watermelon.) List on chalkboard or overhead projector.

- Bulletin Board. Cover a bulletin board with white drawing paper. At the top write "Red" in manuscript letters. Have each of the children draw a red object.

- Read book and view film, *The Red Balloon*.[133]

- Things that can be red: A red wagon, a red sailboat; a red sunset; a red apple; a red flower (rose; hibiscus; geranium; poinsettia; red lily); a red truck; a red car; a red schoolhouse; a red barn; the inside of a watermelon; strawberries; red plums; red grapes; red cabbage; a red rooster; a red dress; a red tie; a red shirt; a red uniform; a traffic light on stop; a stop sign; a redfish; a redbird (a cardinal).

- *The Mystery of the Missing Red Mitten*. My very favorite of the many books by talented author-illustrator Steven Kellogg. The detailed black-and-white drawings are enhanced with at least one splash of "red" on every page.

red
rojo

Sign "red" (courtesy of Gallaudet University, Washington, D.C.).

"WHAT COLOR?"

[Leader Begins:]

Red, red, red, red,

Who is wearing red today?

Red, red, red, red,

Who is wearing red?

[All children with red showing say:]

I am wearing red today.

Look at me and you will say

Red, red, red, red,

I am wearing red.

[Repeat game until most of the basic colors are used.]

Yellow

• Game: Who is wearing yellow? (See words for red on page 111, "What Color?") Red, blue, and green are one-syllable words so the rhythm can be clapped in four: 1, 2, 3, 4. For YELLOW, orange, and purple, vary the words to fit the two-syllable word. Instead of repeating the word four times, just say: "Yellow, yellow," twice. Clap the rhythm and it will be easy! Smile!

Yellow, Yellow (Leader begins)

Who is wearing yellow?

Yellow, Yellow,

Who's in Yellow?

I am wearing yellow (Children stand and respond),

I'm a happy fella,

Yellow, yellow,

I'm in yellow.

• Poem. Read the poem "A Great

Gray Elephant" on page 97. Ask: "What is yellow?" ("a little yellow bee.")

• Read the Mother Goose rhyme about "Daffy-Down-Dilly" (page 10). Ask the children to listen for what's yellow? (Answer: "A bright yellow gown.") See the question about the riddle, page 21.

yellow
amarillo

Sign "yellow" (courtesy of Gallaudet University, Washington, D.C.).

Blue

• Who is wearing blue?

(A leader begins by saying, then asking:)
Blue, blue, blue, blue.
Who is wearing blue today?
(The children wearing blue clothes answer by standing and saying:)
I am wearing blue!
Note: See all of the words on page 111 substituting blue for red.

• Gaze at nature. Choose a sunny day with a bright blue sky and puffy white clouds for your sky gazing. Take the book *Dreams* by Peter

Spier. Encourage the children to gaze at the sky and pretend the clouds are various shapes. Read *It Looks Like Spilt Milk*, Charles Shaw.

- TV-Video. There's a popular TV show for preschoolers using this color word (*Blue's Clues*). The host is like a modern "Mr. Rogers." He talks to a blue dog. On the show are segments to help young children have fun while learning.

- Read Poems: Read "I'm Glad," page 96. Listen for what's blue? (The sky is painted blue.) Read "A Great Gray Elephant," page 97. Listen for the phrase that has blue. (A blue sea.)

blue
azul

Sign "blue" (courtesy of Gallaudet University, Washington, D.C.).

Green

- Who is wearing green?
  (A leader begins by saying:)
  Green, green, green, green.
  Who is wearing green today?
  Green, green, green, green.
  Who is wearing green?
  (All children wearing green stand and say:)

I am wearing green today.
Look at me and you will say
Green, green, green, green,
I am wearing green!

- Nature walk. Instruct everyone to find something green and bring it back to class from a nature walk. Ideas: A green blade of grass or a leaf.

- Read poems: Read "Color Green!" page 113. Read "A Great Gray Elephant," page 97. Listen for the phrase that has green. (A tall green tree.) Read "I'm Glad," page 96. Listen for what's green? (The earth is painted green.)

Color Green!

Green is everywhere.

Observe; look around;

Varied shades of green

Can be found.

Different types of

Plants, trees, and vines

Besides ferns and grasses

Of all kinds.

Look for green!

—G.M. Caughman

Orange

- PUZZLE. "I am a fruit. I am also a

green
verde

Sign "green" (courtesy of Gallaudet University, Washington, D.C.).

color word. What am I? Answer: An orange orange!

- Orange smiles. For a morning snack or an afternoon treat serve "Orange Smiles" when you are studying the color "orange." See food and recipes, page 149.

- Poem. Read the poem "Breakfast." Have children listen for the word orange. (The teeth bite down into the soft, pale-orange fruit … cantaloupe!") This poem will probably be too hard for preschoolers to understand. Use with second and third graders. See page 98.

- Game: Who is Wearing Orange? (See changes for the two-syllable word orange in game, page 112). Game played with a leader and the class of children.

- Vegetable snack. Orange carrot sticks or carrots sliced like coins make a nutritious snack while studying the color orange. Or cook "Soft Carrots" and serve with a toothpick or plastic fork. See recipes on pages 155–156.

- Orange Zest. Do you know the wonderful kitchen tool known as a "zester"?[134] Rub the tool across a lemon or orange and scrape off some of the rind. It's called zest!

  Wash oranges and hands. Let each child taste a pinch of orange zest. Or let children scrape their own.

orange
anaranjado

Sign "orange" (courtesy of Gallaudet University, Washington, D.C.).

Violet

- Puzzle. "I am a color. I am also a tiny flower. What am I?" Answer: A violet violet!

- Purple grapes. For a delicious snack freeze grapes and eat for an icy treat. Children will enjoy.

- Game: Who is wearing violet? Decide on the color word violet or purple for this game. (See changes for the two-syllable word in the game, page 112.) Game played with a leader and the class of children.

- Poem. Read poem "A Great Gray Elephant," p 97. Have the children listen for something violet. (A tiny purple violet.") Note: Here you have the color word and the flower word together.

- Flowers. Real and artificial. Use one or all of these when you study the color violet: Buy pretty bunches of silk violets. Get a purple African Violet for your classroom while studying purple. If native to your area, search for wild violets in the schoolyard. We have them in my Louisiana yard.

- Purple picture. Read to preschoolers the simple storybook *Harold and the Purple Crayon* by Crockett Johnson. Afterward give out sheets of paper to each child. Ask them to get out *only* a purple crayon and draw a purple picture. Help write names on each paper as needed.

- The letter V. Use a purple crayon to make a large violet letter "V" in the center of a blank piece of paper. Have the children each make a similar sheet. Then have them draw all the things they can that are violet or purple.

- Purple ink. Buy a purple ballpoint pen. Write each child's name on a school paper in purple sometime during the week you study purple.

- Sign purple. Begin the sign for the color purple by making the letter "P." Then shake your hand.

- Read Lilly. For more than the color purple read the picture book *Lilly's Purple Plastic Purse* by Kevin Henks. The charming tale recites Lilly's school adventures. Besides the delightful alliteration of "P" in the title, teachers and children will enjoy Lilly's story.

purple
morado

Sign "purple" (courtesy of Gallaudet University, Washington, D.C.).

Lilly's Purple Plastic Purse by Kevin Hanks. N.Y.: Greenwillow, 1996. Full-color art. Many small pictures with watercolor paints and black pen.

DENNIS THE MENACE

"JOEY! WHAT ARE YOU LOOKING FOR?"

"DENNIS SAYS YOU HAVE EYES IN THE BACK OF YOUR HEAD."

9

Rhythm of Play

Toys: The Tools of Play[135]

Teachers in schools, home schools, and day care centers may need this list from the American Toy Institute for guidance in safely buying toys or to distribute to parents. Children of all ages need a well-balanced assortment of toys. Consider the maturity, skill level and interests of children when purchasing toys. For babies and young children carefully consider these safety considerations from the American Toy Institute.

Safety Watch[136]

- Avoid toys with small parts that could be swallowed or sucked into airways.

- Watch for small parts that could be inserted into the nose or ears.

- Check stuffed animals and dolls to determine that eyes and noses are securely fastened and seams are well sewn.

- Choose rattles, teething rings and squeeze toys that cannot even in their most compressed state become lodged in a baby's throat.

- Avoid latex balloons, which frighten babies and present a choking and suffocation hazard.

- Select unbreakable toys that are lightweight, washable, and free of sharp corners, rough edges or strings.

Play Is a Child's Work

Play is universal. Play is a child's work. Even so for babies. Human babies are totally dependent on adults for care. Talk and coo and sing to babies and watch them respond. "How many days has baby to play?" asks the nursery rhyme? See page 6. Every day! Repeat the rhyme as you care for babies and watch them respond. Parents, teachers, and childcare workers can talk, hum, and sing as you feed, bathe, and change babies. Eating, sleeping, crying, and filling diapers are all serious work for babies. So are smiling, laughing, and playing. Notice the rhythms of play.

Babies first play with what's available ... their mouth, hands, feet, and toes.

Toys for Babies Birth to 6 Months[137]

Mobiles: Remove from crib when baby is five months old or is able to push up on hands and knees; musical chime toys; soft cloth toys; soft dolls; stuffed animals with short pile; small safe rattles; bells; balls; squeaky toys; teething toys; cloth and cardboard picture books

Toys for Babies Age 6 Months to 1 Year[138]

Balls 1¾" and larger; push-pull toys; busy boxes; nesting and stacking toys; simple shape sorters; pop-up toys; soft blocks; bath toys; teething toys; large, interlocking rings or keys; soft dolls;

Previous page: *"Dennis the Menace" by Hank Ketcham, used by permission.*

stuffed animals; simple musical instruments; rattles; squeeze-squeak toys; cloth and cardboard picture books.

Toys for Babies Age 1 to 2 Years

According to the American Toy Institute: "In the second year of life, children are explorers. Fueled by curiosity and wonder, toddlers also possess the physical skills that make it easy for them to play and learn. A busy toddler needs toys for physical play — walking, climbing, pushing and riding — and toys that encourage experimentation and manipulation. At this age children imitate adults and enjoy props that help them master life skills."[139]

Balls 1¾" and larger; push-pull toys; ride-on toys propelled by feet; wagons; backyard gym equipment; infant swing, small slide, small climbing apparatus; nesting and stacking toys; simple shape sorters; pop-up toys; puzzles with knobs; whole object pieces; blocks; sandbox and sand toys; wading pool and water toys; bath toys; stuffed animals; dolls and baby gear; play vehicles; kitchen equipment and gadgets; play household items — telephone, lawn mower, workbench, shopping cart; playhouse; child-sized table and chairs; non-toxic art supplies; large crayons; clay; finger paints; musical instruments; cardboard picture books; pop-up books.

Toys for Babies Ages 2 to 3 Years[140]

All of the items in list for ages 1 to 2 years plus:

Books; building blocks and building systems; blocks with letters and numbers; dolls that can be fed, bathed, and diapered; dress-up clothes and accessories; hand and finger puppets; art supplies; add sidewalk chalk; tricycle and helmet; play scenes; farm, airport, service station with figures and accessories.

Games for Babies Birth to 3 Years

Peek-a-boo; Pat-a-Cake; Wave bye-bye! Make sounds. Try words. Touch objects and textures. Try to stand. Stand, crawl, and then walk. Stack blocks. Put objects in containers. Hear rhymes, poems. Sing.

Finger Plays, Songs, Games, Riddles

PEEKABOO!

Does everyone know how to play this game? Daddies, aunts and grandparents can have delightful play with babies and young children. Did you know the word "peekaboo" is in the dictionary?

Some say "Peep-pie, Boo!" You will hear variations and may choose to make up your own. We have a precious story in our family about our daughter playing "Peekaboo" with the baby in the manger under the Christmas tree!

As defined by *Webster's* the game is played "to amuse a young child, in which someone hides his face, as behind his hands, and then suddenly reveals it, calling, 'Peekaboo!"[141]

If you've never played this game with a young child, find one today, play and watch their face!

Games and Play for Preschoolers

Play for Three Year Olds

"Imaginative play begins in the third year," according to the American Toy Institute.[142]

Balls, boxes, beanbags, blocks, and books!; books, books, books!; strings and big beads!; modeling clay; colorful art papers: construction paper, tissue paper, colored craft paper; jars of bubbles, bubble wands; watercolor paints, brushes, and large sheets of paper; finger-paint; large crayons and large sheets of paper; puzzles with large pieces; play clothes box; home life area (anything used at home to "Play House" or "Play Mam-ma and Dad-dy"; dishes, dustmop, dolls, blanket-squares); musical rhythm instruments (see page 127); recorded music (instrumental, singing accompaniments, cassettes and CDs); riding toys: tricycle, fire-truck, car, and truck, school bus; wagons; sand table (inside) and sandbox (outside), various sizes of seashells; stick horse; a mirror.

BLOW BUBBLES

Gift. "I'm forever blowing bubbles..." children sing while waving bubble-wands in the air. I loved blowing bubbles as a child and still love to give "bubbles" as a birthday gift to young children. The fragile effervescent bubbles sparkle in the sunshine as they float upward, up and up. Plan a delightful inexpensive school activity as a gift to your children. Enjoy the simple gift of blowing soap bubbles together and watching pretty bubbles in the air!

Use bubble ideas:

- Buy small jars of bubbles with plastic wands included for each child. Ask for school funds or help from parent groups for the purchase.

- You may prefer to make your own bubble mix. Enlist another faculty member or a parent volunteer to help you make bubble mix in quantity. See recipe on page 120.

- Blow bubbles in springtime on the playground at recess.

- Blow bubbles at a picnic on the school grounds.

- Blow bubbles on a school field trip to the park, zoo or other outing.

- Give portions of bubble mix to all students at a school-wide Spring Fun Fair. Look in your library for Tana Hoban's book *Round and Round*. Find the beautiful photograph of two children blowing soap bubbles.

- Wrap a small jar of bubbles in red paper in December or February for a Christmas or Valentine's gift for each child.

Hints for Enjoying Bubbles: Bubbles love high humidity. For dry days or low humidity add more water to the recipe. Wind can sometimes cause problems for your fragile bubbles. Cloudy days are good for bubbles. But you can have success with bubbles on sunny days. On hot days cool your bubble solution in the shade. See a recipe for a quantity of bubble solution on page 120.

Recipe: Bubble Solution
— Cathy Dennis and author

Basic Proportions: 1:10
Joy dishwashing liquid
Lukewarm water
Glycerin (optional)

Using these basic proportions you can make *any* amount of bubble solution. The proportion is: one part of soap liquid to ten parts of water. See hints for blowing bubbles on page 119.

DIRECTIONS: Mix 1 cup Joy liquid detergent with 10 cups of lukewarm water. On very dry days, add 10 percent to 50 percent more water. (For more durable bubbles, add 3-4 Tablespoons glycerin.) Use bubble wand and blow bubbles.

Caution: Recommended for bubbles are Joy or Dawn detergents. In some water, clear Ivory liquid works. Some dishwashing liquids will not work at all. Try your brand at home before making bubbles at school. The glycerin is optional, available at Wal-Mart Pharmacy. Your hand can be a bubble wand. Cup hand placing thumb and index finger together forming a circle, dip into bubble solution, and blow softly. Use a plastic wand. Or shape wire coat-hangers to form wands.

Play for Four Year Olds[143]

All of the list for three-year olds plus: more balls, boxes, and books!; jump-rope; swing, slide, jungle gym, stick horse; modeling clay; art paper and scissors; soap bubbles; watercolor paints, brushes, and large sheets of paper; finger-paint; large crayons and large sheets of paper; puzzles with large pieces; dress-up clothes box; a mirror; home living area; musical rhythm instruments (add drums); recorded music (instrumental, singing accompaniments, cassettes and CDs); wagons and riding toys (tricycle, fire-truck, car, truck or school bus); sand table (inside) and sandbox (outside); large seashells; lightweight tools; flashlight; building blocks with pieces for creative play: (towers, arches, squares, and rectangles); hand puppets; kites (with help).

GAME: SHOES ARE RIGHT?

A Dilemma for Children: Are Shoes Right or Wrong?

In learning to dress themselves, children often put their shoes or slippers on the wrong feet. A question mark follows the name of this game: "Shoes Are Right?" The question means are shoes on the correct feet? Is each shoe on the correct foot?

An easy way to teach children the correct way to put on their shoes is to put the two shoes together and look at them carefully. Ask:

- Q: Are shoes right or wrong?

- Q: Do the shoes point straight ahead, *Andrew*? (Add names)

- Q: Or do the shoes turn outward? A: Shoes straight ahead is right. The correct way. (Teach children the word "correct" in the context.) A: Shoes outward is wrong!

MAKE A GAME

MATERIALS: Poster-board. Laminating material. Pair of small shoes to trace around. Pair of adult shoes, size 12, to use with game. Two labeled pictures with captions.

OPTIONAL: A tall child-sized mirror.

DIRECTIONS: Make a game for younger children. Reproduce these shoes with labels. Have one picture that is (right) correct and one picture that is wrong. Draw arrows as shown:

OPTIONAL: You may want to highlight the inside arch (shown here with dots) with a bright color.

Make these labels:

1. "What's wrong with this picture?" Shoes are wrong!

2. "Shoe game: Shoes are correct!"

Laminate posters if possible. Or cover with clear adhesive paper.

GAMES

Place the two laminated posters on the floor with a large pair of shoes. Children will laugh putting their feet into the large shoes. Children can quickly see if toes are straight ahead (correct) or turned outward (wrong) on large shoes. Then let them place their own feet on top of the "Poster Feet."

OPTIONAL: A tall mirror for children to see themselves would be an enjoyable addition to this game.

Read *Shoes* by William Joyce.

Recite this rhyme:

Rhyme: My Shoes

I can put my two shoes on
I think I'm very neat
I place the two shoes side by side
And slip in my two feet.

— G.M. Caughman

Correct.

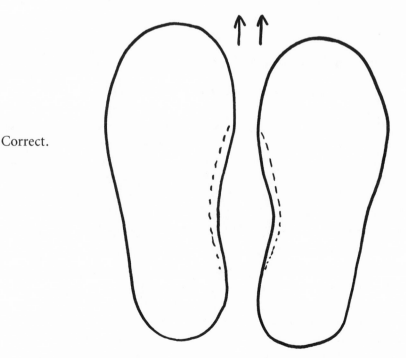

"Josiah's Correct Shoes" by author.

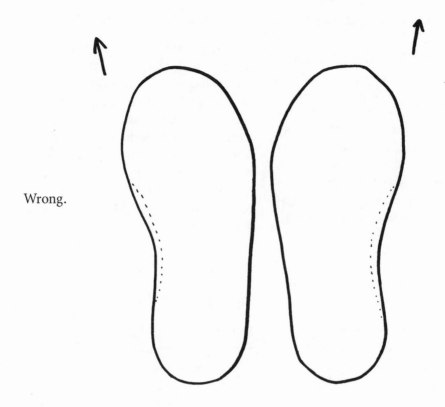

Wrong.

"Andrews' Wrong Shoes" by author.

Games and Play for Kindergarten and First Graders

Play for Five-Year-Olds

Books!; beads and blocks; more balls, boxes, and books!; jump-rope; simple board games and easy card games; swing, slide, jungle gym, stick horse; developing friendships; playing with friends; modeling clay; art paper and scissors; soap bubbles; finger-paint; watercolor paints, brushes, and large sheets of paper; large crayons and large sheets of paper; puzzles; simple riddles and silly jokes; dress-up clothes box (be sure to include a mirror!); home living area; homemaking equipment (includ-

ing cleaning and cooking supplies); "play-like": playing doctor, nurse, teacher, preacher, carpenter, astronaut, engineer or policewoman (any profession in your community or in the child's world); dolls, doll clothes, doll buggy, dollhouses; musical rhythm instruments; recorded music: instrumental, singing accompaniments, cassettes and CDs; riding toys: wagon, tricycle, firetruck, car, and truck, school bus, scooter; toys with wheels: trains, trucks, tractors, bulldozers; sand table (inside and outside), sandbox (outside), various sizes of seashells; lightweight tools; flashlight; workbench; building blocks (with towers, arches, squares, and rectangles); puppets (puppet stages, simple finger puppets, bag puppets, sock puppets); miniatures (villages, farms, service stations, space stations, or ranches — animals, and people); skates (roller skates and ice-skates); kites; punching bag; nature and science objects and materials (magnifying glass, magnets, abalone shell, prism, peacock feathers); clock (be sure to have a clock with hands, not a digital one in the classroom!); water play (as appropriate).

"What's in the Bag?"

Preparation:

- Buy a package of small brown paper bags

- Label bag: "What's in the Bag?"

- Gather objects to identify

- Put several common objects in paper-bag. *Suggestions*: bar of soap; paper clip; kitchen teaspoon; small rubber ball.

Play Game:

1. The game is simple. Ask a child to put hand in bag and without looking, identify the object by touch. Let other children try to identify objects.

2. After individual children have tried to guess, say: "What's in the Bag? Let's see!" Take objects out of the bag one at the time. As you show each item to the class have them identify the object responding in unison.

Introduce Books:

You can use the game "What's in the Book?" to introduce books by Tana Hoban. Show photos from books and have class make identifications in unison. See examples on page 124.

Play Games with Shapes!

Make puzzles and games of various shapes. Play sight recognition games. Just as children can learn to name letters and numbers without complete comprehension, so they can learn to name and recognize shapes. Sight recognition and configuration are part of reading readiness. Before children make discoveries in the branch of mathematics called geometry they can have fun learning shapes by playing.

Shapes, Patterns, Forms

Note: Actually geometry is my favorite branch of mathematics! There are professions in which knowledge of geometry is essential. If you find children with an interest in more, take them to the library. There's always more to read and learn. Explore angles, planes, points, lines, surfaces and solids. Have fun with forms, patterns, and shapes.

Preparation:

Reproduce the shapes you need. Choose from these materials:

- Colored paper
- Sandpaper
- Wood
- Poster board
- Cardboard
- Adhesive paper
- Thin sheets of foam
- Cold gelatin!

(You can refrigerate pans of thin gelatin. Use cookie cutters to make gelatin shapes for lesson plans or holiday themes!)

Shapes!

BOOKS ABOUT SHAPES

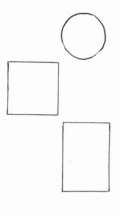

"Shapes" by author.

Tana Hoban's concept books[144] are well known to nursery school and kindergarten teachers. Since she keeps her concepts simple the books are also used by teachers of children who have emotional, mental, or physical handicaps. Show children the photographs in these books when studying shapes. Or use the books as a game anytime:

- *Round and Round and Round* (Greenwillow, 1983). Let children identify the things that are round. Swiss cheese is fun. There is a beautiful photograph of two children blowing round soap bubbles.

- *Shapes, Shapes, Shapes* (Greenwillow, 1986). Besides all the shapes pictured in this chapter, Hoban also asks children to look for these "shapes": arc, heart, and stars.

- *Spirals, Curves, Fanshapes, and Lines* (Greenwillow, 1992) will introduce children to geometry. Not for the very young child, these are more difficult concepts than most of Hoban's books.

Play for Six to Nine Years

The American Toy Institute states, "School-age children enjoy play that requires strategy and skill."[145] Favorites include: board games, tabletop sports, and classic toys such as marbles, yo-yos, jump ropes, and kites. Grade-schoolers also enjoy seeking information and experiences through play. They like exploring and learning through science and craft kits. These ages possess the physical skills and coordination to enjoy junior versions of some adult sports equipment. Game and toy suggestions for grade schoolers are:

- Easy-to-read books ; animal stories; some children's classics. Still enjoy being read to.

- Classic toys: Jump ropes, yo-yos, marbles, kites, balls.

- Art supplies: Paint, Crayons (all kinds), easel, clay.

- Board games.

- Science sets, model kits, craft kits.

- Construction toys.

- Tape player and tapes.

- Gym equipment.

- Bicycle and helmet.

- Sports equipment: Baseball glove, ball, bat; hockey stick; tennis racket, balls; football; protective gear for all hobbies and sports.

- Skates: Ice skates; roller skates or roller blades; protective gear.

- Construction toys.

- Dolls: Paper dolls, fashion and career dolls, puppets, doll houses and furnishings.

- Electronic games.

- Jigsaw puzzles.

- Video games.

MORE SHAPES:

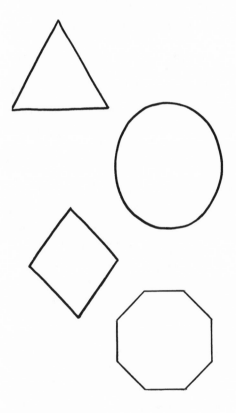

"Shapes" by author.

A Poem as Play

You can certainly *play* with Shel Silverstein's poems. Read one of these until you find a favorite poem or drawing. Then play with your children via poems.

- *Where the Sidewalk Ends*

- *A Light in the Attic*

Read Silverstein's poems from your favorite volume of his several books and you will think of many more playful ideas with poetry. Here's a favorite poem I have used for many years: "Love" by Shel Silverstein (from *Where the Sidewalk Ends*, Harper and Row, 1974).

PREPARATION: Prepare a large letter "V." Make the letter bright red or decorate with hearts. Mount on a popsicle stick or place the letter in your personal book as a bookmark at the place of the poem "Love."

IN CLASS:

1. Hold the letter "V" in one hand and the open book in the other.

2. Slowly read the short poem "Love" by Shel Silverstein.

3. Ask for a volunteer to come hold up the letter "V" and act-out the words as you re-read the poem.

Cut-out the following letter "V" from colorful gift wrap, wallpaper, or art paper. Leave as it is or enlarge, decorate and glue to a plain 4" × 6" index card.

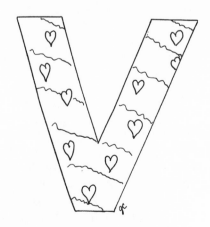

"V" in Love by author.

Inexpensive Games

No money for buying toys and games? Games don't have to be expensive. Children can entertain themselves with boxes, string, sticks, paper, anything! Encourage imaginative play.

1. Bowls and a Ball. Take six unbreakable bowls and one small ball to school. Line up the bowls in rows like this:

    x x x   Three across the back
     x x   Two across the middle
      x   One in the front

Let children take turns standing back on a line. Toss ball toward bowls.

The child filling the bowls the most times wins.

Note: For older children, designate points for various bowls.

2. Bottles and a Ball. Gather a collection of soft drink bottles or cans. Line them up. Let the children take turns rolling the ball on the floor, pavement, or ground like a bowling ball and knocking over the bottles.

3. Redlight Stop!

- Children line up horizontally, facing one child who is the policeman.

- The policeman, who is a distance away, covers eyes and counts out loud to ten (from 1 to 10).

- As soon as the policeman's eyes are covered the children run toward him trying to reach him.

- When the policeman reaches "ten" he opens eyes and calls out: "Redlight! Stop!" Any child who is moving at all has to go back to the beginning line.

- The first child who reaches the policeman to "tag him" wins the game and becomes "it."

- The game begins again with the winner as the policeman or woman.

4. Boxes. Get an assortment of cardboard boxes. Businesses crush or recycle them. Have a creative playtime or art activity where children "play" with the boxes. Let their imaginations go. They will make playhouses, clubhouses, forts, trains, airplanes, trucks, stores, spaceships, and a dozen other things. If available, provide crayons or markers.

5. Play outside games. Children enjoy outside games such as hopscotch (draw design in dirt with a stick), jump rope, softball. For dodge ball: Everyone is in the middle except ones on each end who throw the ball. If the ball touches anyone they are out. The last one in wins.

6. Play inside mental games. Rainy day? Or need a break in your routine? Play some inside games: guessing games such as "I Spy" (choose a color and let everyone take turns guessing where it is in plain sight); puzzles such as "How many words can you make from this word?" (for second and third graders); riddles (young children enjoy funny jokes and silly riddles); and "Simon Says" (like "Follow the Leader" except each time the leader says "Simon Says"). Hint: Establish rules **before** game begins.

7. Make simple musical instruments and play them. Have children save materials at home you will use on a certain date. Remind them to bring to school. Provide a few extras.

- Drums. Make drums from round cardboard oatmeal or grits containers. Place rocks or shells inside. Tape shut. Cover with paper or paint. Let dry. Play.

- Tambourines. Tie on metal bottle caps around the edge of aluminum pie pans.

- Water glasses. Fill glasses with water at various levels. Play with spoons.

- Button on a string. Thread string through button forming a loop. Tie. Twirl for "twang" sound. Simple and fun.

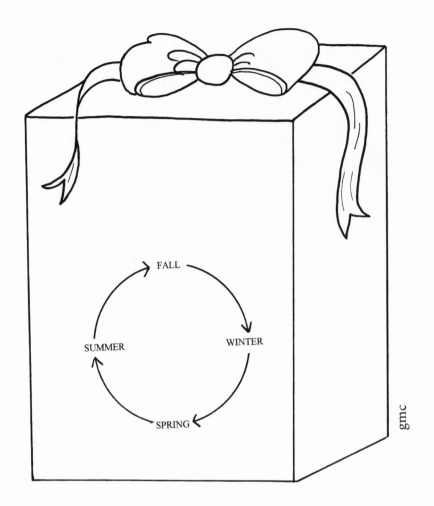

FALL

WINTER

SUMMER

SPRING

gmc

10

Rhythm of Seasons

New School Year Activities
August-September

Helping Hands

"Helping Hands" could be a school-wide theme for a month or a year. Children enjoy helping. Give them opportunity with various chores. In each classroom, specific helping assignments can be given. Rotate the jobs throughout the year to give all the children a turn performing all of the tasks. Good classroom management idea. Consider the needs of your classroom and compile a list.

CLASSROOM DUTIES

Water plants	Feed goldfish
Erase chalkboard	Feed turtle
Dust erasers	Feed gerbil
Clean dust-less boards	Feed (other pets)
Errands for the teacher	Line leader
Pick up school mail	

HELPING HANDS ACTIVITIES

- Let each child draw around hand. Write first name on hand.

- Prepare helping chart. Choose from these options:

    1. List duties on a poster with slits underneath the size of child's wrist. Prepare a "hand" of each child. Place the child of the week in poster.

    2. Make a chart of clear vinyl with pockets. Sew on machine. Write chores and place in pockets.

    3. Buy a clear door-hanging shoe bag and use as above. Make signs. Insert hands. Change weekly. See illustration.

    4. Buy clear hanging jewelry pockets.

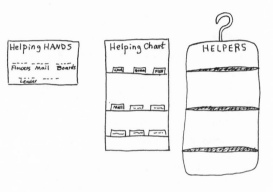

"Helping Hands" by the author.

- Teach the community of your class to share work and be helpful.

NAME TAGS

Name tags and place cards have a place in the classroom of the young child year round. In the beginning of the year you will be helping each child with sight recognition of their own name by preparing a name tag for them to wear and a name sign for his designated desk space. Room labels will also be helpful to the child such as: teacher; desk; chalkboard; flag. Add other signs such as: books, pencil sharpener; dictionary; wastebasket; window; light ... (others in your room).

Opposite page: *"A Gift"— Rhythm of Seasons by the author.*

Learning to recognize, spell, and write one's own name is an important task.

Name tags and place cards will also help children learn the names of others in their classroom. Use manuscript lettering, upper and lower case for proper names. Children will learn names by sight recognition and by the configuration of the word. Sample name tages on pages 77, 96, 136, 138.

Make a "Face on a Stick" Yellow Happy Face/Blue Sad Face

Make a visual aid to use at various times during the school year.

DIRECTIONS: Prepare faces on a stick using these directions:

1. Cut one large yellow circle and one large blue circle from construction paper or poster board. (Make the circles four to six inches in diameter.) These circles will eventually form your faces on a stick.

2. Draw a smiling face on the yellow circle and a sad face on the blue circle. If possible, laminate the faces.

3. Place the two faces back to back, face out. Mount part of the stick inside the two faces like a spine, gluing the stick and faces together.

4. The yellow face in the front is smiling. Turn it over and the blue face is frowning.

Suggestions for teaching with young children:

- Start the day by holding up the yellow side. Sing "Good Morning to You," page 80 or "How I Love to Sing," page 70.

- When part of the class acts grumpy, take your "Faces on a Stick" and say: "A smile is a frown turned upside down!" Ask, "Which looks better?" Show blue side but quickly turn back to yellow side.

- Read several of Charlotte Zolotow's books about feelings (*The Quarreling Book*. N.Y.: Harper and Row, 1963, by Charlotte Zolotow, pictures by Arnold Lobel). Have a child volunteer to hold the "Stick Faces" and show the feelings and attitudes in the book as you read *The Quarreling Book*.

- Discuss good manners.

Crowns

Make a crown of tissue paper and keep nearby in your desk. During the rhythms of the seasons and events of the year you'll find many uses. A garland or wreath was worn on the head as a sign of honor or victory. A champion in sports earned a garland or wreath as a reward or honor for merit. A monarch wore a circlet or headdress of gold and jewels as an emblem of sovereignty. A person became a monarch by putting a crown on his or her head. Kings and queens

"A Crown" by author.

wear crowns. Have fun with paper crowns in your classroom.

Make at least one tissue paper crown to have on hand. These simple crowns can have variety by the colors and designs of tissue paper you use. Make crowns in white, primary colors, jewel tones, or pastels. Use colorful designs for storytime, birthdays, Valentine's Day, Christmas, or any celebration. Celebrate "Today." Make any day an occasion.

MAKE A CROWN

DIRECTIONS:

1. Take two pieces of tissue paper approximately 12" long and 5" wide. Place one perfectly on top of the other. Glue ends together.

2. Fold in half lengthwise. Then fold each end so they perfectly overlap. The folded paper is about 2" wide and 5" high.

3. Get a pair of scissors. Start at top edge and cut at a 45 degree angle to the other edge. (See illustration.) Note: You are only making one simple cut.

4. Unfold your crown. Your crown has 6 points. Optional: Decorate with small stars or hearts. Remember, the tissue paper is lightweight.

Folded paper to cut crown.

MORE IDEAS FOR USING CROWNS

1. Have a crown for a king and queen and prince and princesses and give everyone in the classroom a title and a crown.

2. Before reading a story containing a king, queen, or other royalty, choose children to wear crowns, sit in a chair (throne) in front of the class and pretend to be these people as you read.

3. Read a familiar fairy tale such as "Cinderella," and then let children act out the story with simple props. Have a crown for the prince and one ready for Cinderella at the end of the story.

4. Make a red crown for all of the children for Valentine's Day. Each child can be either a Queen of Hearts or a King of Hearts. Add lightweight heart sequins of a contrasting color to the edge of the crown.

5. Honor a birthday child with a crown for the day. Sing "Happy Birthday to You." See song, page 81.

6. On Friday choose a boy and a girl to be king and queen who have been the model of excellent behavior all week. Have a crowning ceremony. Let them line up first to go home wearing their crown.

7. Before Christmas let all the children wear a crown for a Christmas party and to sing Christmas carols. Three gifts were brought by the "wise men" of the biblical Christmas story. There may have been many men. Have an entire room of wise boys and girls at your Christmas holiday celebration. (See Matthew 2.)

8. Welcome the New Year with a "Back to School Celebration." Ease back

into your school schedule in January. Ask one child to be Max. Write the name "Max" in black letters on a gold paper crown. Let "Max" sit before the class as you read the modern classic of children's literature, *Where the Wild Things Are* (Sendak). Afterward discuss what was real and imagined. Let children draw pictures of the story. Post pictures on one wall or on a bulletin board with the caption: "Happy New Year, Max!" Now the bulletin board you left empty for the Christmas holidays has something on it your first day back from vacation.

The First "R": Reading Rhythms

Schools are about reading readiness, learning to read, and reading. Read, read, read to your students. Read aloud every day. Utilize these logos and illustrations on bulletin boards, posters, overhead-projector transparencies, bookmarks, notes to parents, in the principal's office, cafeteria, and yardsigns.

- Illustration: "The Joy of Reading."

- Illustration: "A Nation of Readers."

- Illustration: "Wake Up and Read."

WAKE UP AND READ!

"*The Joy of Reading*" *(courtesy Library of Congress, Center for the Book).*

Top: "*Wake Up and Read*" *(courtesy ALA)*; Bottom: *Postage Stamp: "A Nation of Readers" "Stamp Design © 1984 U.S. Postal Service. Reproduced with permission. All rights Reserved.*

Fall Rhythms:
October and November

- In September, October, or November, plan a unit "On the Farm," "Fall Harvest," or "Our Fruits and Vegetables." Visit a farm, apple orchard, or a pumpkin patch. Arrange to pick apples or choose pumpkins. Research what's available in your area. Make a simple pumpkin or another type pie.

- Autumn Display. Buy one large bright-orange pumpkin or use several sizes of pumpkins to decorate your library or classroom. Select pumpkins that are firm and sit flat on the bottom. Buy colorful ornamental gourds and pots of mums (nickname for chrysanthemums). Arrange attractively. Add hay bales for an unusual seating for your storytime.

- Read aloud Lucille Clifton's poem "October" from *Everett Anderson's Year*.

- Pumpkin Hints. You may choose to draw or carve a face on your pumpkin in October. Select the side you will use as the front. Draw a simple face with permanent felt-tip markers. Make two triangle eyes, one triangle for a nose and a large crescent mouth. You may add a smiling snaggletooth. The Pumpkin top: Cut out the top like a hat. Cut the pumpkin's lid at an angle so it won't fall through. Lift the hat off and scoop out the seeds and pulp. Scoop from the bottom up and scrape until the inside is clean. Be sure to remove all the fibrous

material. Carve face: You may choose to carve a face as a treat for children. For a simple face, draw with markers before you cut. For an intricate carved design, use small blades from a carving kit available in hardware stores. Place a glass votive cup inside the pumpkin as a candleholder. Rub cinnamon on the pumpkin's lid. As the candle burns you will have a luscious, pumpkin-pie smell![146]

- Read-Aloud. My favorite Halloween story to read aloud to young children is Charlotte Zolotow's *A Tiger Called Thomas*. Though the story setting is the end of October, these concerns are addressed: Loneliness, low self-esteem, shyness, and friendship. First read the story for enjoyment. Make or buy a tiger mask and put in front of your face. Discuss Thomas' feelings and actions. Ask, "Is the tiger in the story real or imagined? "Ask: "Are you friendly?" Then state: "The way to have friends is to be friendly."

- The colorful book, *The Trip* by Ezra Jack Keats, is set at Halloween. Or read *The Trek* by Ann Jonas.

- For preschoolers, try Eric Carle's *Watch Out! A Giant*. The author-illustrator said he created this book as an introduction for the very young to the world of fairy tales.

- Fall Festival. Plan a school-wide Fall Festival. Have children come to school as friendly Mother Goose and nursery rhyme characters instead of wearing scary costumes. See list of characters, pages 18–19.

- Fears. Read a pair of poems by Eloise Greenfield, show the pictures by Gilchrist and discuss real and imagined fears: 1) "The House with the Wooden Windows" and 2) "Darnell (both from *Night on Neighborhood Street*).

- Celebrate Children's Book Week. Read stories. Plan a School-wide Book Character Dress-Up Day. See pages 15–16.

- Bears! Plan a library, classroom, or school-wide bears day! Let every child bring their favorite teddy bear to school. Choose from these ideas: (1) Have a Teddy Bear's Parade at recess. (2) Play the music "Teddy Bear's Picnic" over the public address system. (3) Have a contest. Decide on a name such as: Prettiest Bear, Most Loved Bear, Funniest Bear. (4) Place three chairs in front of the class as props. Let children act out the story of "The Three Bears." (5) Read bear stories. There are dozens! (6) Buy bear cookies for snacks. (7) Invite parents for a "Teddy Bear's Picnic." (8) Use bear name tags for parents, page 96. (9) Use the bear theme for Grandparents Day. (10) Celebrate bears for Children's Book Week or National Library Week.

- Autumn Artwork: Make a Leaf Man (glue a leaf on a page as the body; draw a head, arms and legs). Mosaic: Cut up bits of colored construction paper and glue onto a page in an original design.

- Make a Cornucopia (Horn of Plenty). Place on a bulletin board. Let children draw and cut out fruit and vegetables to fill to overflowing.

- Community Helpers: Parents, Grocer, Postal Worker, Farmer, Doctor, Nurse, Teacher, Fireman, Preacher, Librarian, Garbage Man, Recycle Man, Carpenter, Banker.

- Bulletin Board: "I am thankful for..." Have children suggest words as you write on the chalkboard. Enlarge Durer's "Praying Hands," page 136. Let each child choose a word they will use in a picture for the Class Bulletin Board. Discuss.

- Class Booklet. Have each child draw or paint a picture for a class Thanksgiving booklet: "We are thankful for..."

- Bulletin Board Caption: "For the Beauty of the Earth" Make pictures of beauty in nature. Trees, mountains, flowers, sky, clouds, swamp, desert, grass, bushes, animals...

- Feature Pilgrims, Indians and the First Thanksgiving. Have ½ children dress as Pilgrims and ½ as Indians. Make white paper Pilgrim collars and Indian headpieces. Place a feather in a paper headband. See the feather on page 136. Make drums from boxes (page 127). Sit in a large circle. Beat "oatmeal box drums." Make up an Indian chant. Use a 1, 2, 3, 4 beat and the syllable: Oh, Oh, Oh, Oh. Change to Yah-yah-yah-yah. Let children choose other sounds. Pretend to grind corn to make cornmeal to make food. Chant, "We are all grinding corn" (see music, page 76). String raw cranberries and popcorn to decorate your classroom. Stick paper feathers fan-shaped in the end of a pineapple turned on its side to form a turkey decoration.

- Word Fun. Choose from: Thanksgiving; Indians; Pilgrims; turkey; pumpkin; maize, cranberries, give thanks, feast, Thank God…

- Make Thanksgiving Artwork: "Turkey Nut Cups," page 137; "Handy Turkeys," page 138; "Apple Turkeys," page 153; Make place cards suggestions, page 137; Make objects from clay: Indian bowls, Water Jars; Pine Cone Turkeys"; "Potato Turkeys;" make a Class Mural: a long picture of: The First Thanksgiving.

- Set Table. Help children learn to set the table so they can thank their mothers by helping set the table at home. See pages 136–137.

- Give each child a tail feather. Tell children to write or draw something they are thankful for. Place a caption on a bulletin board: "Our Thankful Turkey." Make a turkey head. Staple tail feathers in a fan shape behind the turkey head.

- Repeat rhythms; Finger plays; and songs. Sing, "Ten Little Indians" and "Ten Little Pilgrims," page 68; Chant, "Grinding Corn," page 76; Finger play: "The Pilgrims," page 136.

- Nature Walk. Go on a nature walk. Pick up nature items natural to your area. Make a "Nature Collage" (a picture made with a number of items grouped together).

- Plan a Thanksgiving Feast and invite parents. Let children sign their name to this invitation:

The Pilgrims came over in 1620
But I want you to come to our school
For a Thanksgiving Feast
On ___ November at __ o'clock.

- Invitation. You could let children cut out the invitation and glue it on the back of a piece of their artwork. For example: A Handy Turkey! See page 138.

- Let children help set the table for the Thanksgiving Feast, page 137.

- Counting. For math and arithmetic readiness and experiences let children count: Objects on Bulletin Board; Toothpicks in turkey's tail of Potato Turkey or count as you sing, "Ten Little Indians" or "… Pilgrims." See pages 67–68.

- Number the Days! Count days on the calendar. As you add each date on the classroom calendar, count the days until Thanksgiving Holiday. Daily count in unison from the beginning of the month to the current day.

- Turkey in the Straw! Hide a cellophane or foil-wrapped chocolate turkey in a dishpan of straw. Let the children take turns trying to find the turkey with a fork.

- Make a class Thanksgiving Card to send to the principal; the school nurse; the janitors; the school secretaries…

- Make place mats and place cards for a school dinner.

Feather Bookmark by John Taube.

The Pilgrims

Here are ten little Pilgrims
    (Hold up both
hands)

Marching along to church
    (Move hands in rhythm to words)

1-2-3-4-5 Pilgrim Men
    (Wave each finger on right hand

1-2-3-4-5 Pilgrim Women
    (Wave each finger on left hand)

Very early in the day
    (Place hands together as folded in
prayer)

Pilgrims often went to pray.

Albrecht Durer's "Praying Hands."

Setting the Table!

Children like to help and need to learn meaningful work and how to be helpful. Make setting the table fun. You can teach children at school the basics of table setting, simple table manners, and the art of table conversation which will

have carryover value into their homes. Very young children can learn to set the table.

Start simply with the youngest children. As your children grow in age and maturity add new experiences:

1. Preschooler. A young toddler can learn to correctly place a plate, cup, spoon, and napkin on the table.

2. Paper place mat. Make a place mat for each child from a large sheet of drawing paper or newsprint.[147]

3. Plastic place mat. In a classroom "Home Living Area" for young children, make a learning tool for them to "play setting the table." On a placemat draw an outline for correct placement of the simplest table setting:

- In the center of the place mat, make a large circle for a plate;

- Draw a small circle to the top right of the plate for the cup or glass;

- To the right of the plate draw a spoon;

- To the left of the plate draw a rectangle for a napkin. See Illustration, page 137.

4. First and second grade children can add these parts to the above directions: Plate in the center of the table setting; spoon to the right with glass above; fork on the left of the plate and napkin to the left of the fork. See Illustration, page 137.

5. By third grade or before, add the knife to the table setting. Children are learning to manage a knife. The proper place for the knife is to the right

of the plate with the sharper blade facing toward the plate.

Three table rules: (1) Really listen to each other! (2) Take turns speaking, eating, and listening! (3) Pleasant talk at the table!

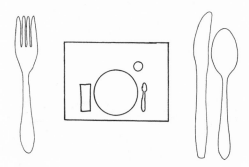

Young children set table.

Setting the table.

Turkey Nut Cups

Let each child make a turkey nut cup to hold nuts or mints. Use on the student's desk; as place favors for a school Thanksgiving Dinner; for a faculty party or to take home for a holiday decoration.

MATERIALS:

A stapler and staples
Small paper nut cups and
Paper cupcake liners
Cut out small red turkey necks

DIRECTIONS:

1. Fold paper cupcake liner over to let the top part show. See Illustration.

2. Let children decorate this folded paper to look like spread turkey feathers.

3. Let child add eyes to each side of turkey head.

4. Staple turkey head to the front of the cup. Illustration.

5. Staple paper "feathers" to the back of the cup.

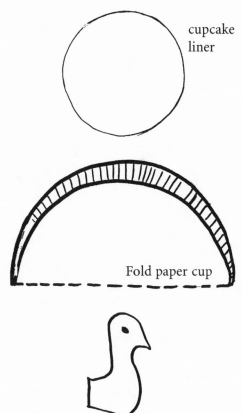

Top: *Cupcake liner;* Middle: *Paper turkey feathers;* Bottom: *Turkey head.*

Hand Turkey!

MATERIALS:
    Paper
    Crayons or felt-tip markers

DIRECTIONS: Let each child have fun making a "Handy Turkey" by using their own hand. Instruct children to place their hand on a sheet of paper with widely spread fingers. The thumb should be turned to face forward to form the head of the turkey. The other four fingers will form the tail feathers of the turkey. Let children trace around their hand.

Show pictures of real turkeys. Let children creatively add an eye, a beak, a wattle, and legs. If they choose they can add to the drawing: Color the feathers; place the turkey in a rural scene, on a farm; or with other turkeys.

Top: *"Hand turkey"*; Bottom: *"Place Cards."*

Winter Rhythms:
December, Christmas, Hanukkah

Play Selections from Tchaikovsky's "Nutcracker"

Sounds of "The Nutcracker Suite" by the Russian composer Tchaikovsky greeted students as they entered my school library for classes two weeks before Christmas holidays. Children and teachers enthusiastically received the lessons and enjoyed the pleasant music.

"Nutcracker" Lesson Plans Objective:

Music appreciation: Introduce classical music selections from Tchaikovsky's "The Nutcracker Suite."

PREPARATION:

• Obtain a recording, tape, or CD of Tchaikovsky's "The Nutcracker Suite."

THE NUTCRACKER

• Print the composer's name and the name of the music both on the chalkboard and on an overhead projector cell (if available).

• Learn the simple story of "The Nutcracker": A little girl opens a Christmas gift she receives and finds a toy nutcracker. She loves the toy and takes it to bed with her. In her dreams the nutcracker is a handsome prince and takes her on a fantasy trip "where she is greeted by the Sugarplum Fairy and entertained with games, dances, and toys."[148]

- Decide which selections, listed below, you will play for each class.
- Read more about Peter Illitch Tchaikovsky (1840–1893) in Chapter 6, on pages 91–92.

METHOD:

- For two weeks before Christmas holidays play the rhythmic selections from "The Nutcracker Suite" each time the students enter the library for classes.

- Turn on the overhead projector with the words listed on the cell: "You are listening to: "The Nutcracker Suite" (or Casse-Noisette) by Peter Ilitch Tchaikovsky, who was a Russian composer of beautiful music. Point to the words on the chalkboard: "The Nutcracker Suite" by Peter Tchaikovsky.

- Play different selections each time children visit. For your information:
  Selections from: "Nutcracker Suite"
  "The Nutcracker Suite" (or Casse-Noisette) by Tchaikovsky:

1. "The Miniature Overture," an introduction to the work.

2. "Dance of the Sugarplum Fairy."

3. "Trepak." Children like the Russian dance with a fast rhythm.

4. "Arab Dance" features a clarinet.

5. A "Chinese Dance" lets the children hear the flute and the piccolo.

6. "The Waltz of the Flowers" is especially lovely in 1, 2, 3 waltz time. You may know a popular song made to this tune, "Come Join the Fun Tonight."

Art by Carol O'Regan.

Smells of Christmas

Plan to have some of these pleasant smells in your library and classroom during the month of December:

- Candles. Candles make a soft glow and give off a pleasing fragrance. Only burn candles if you can do so safely.

  Caution: Never leave candles burning unattended! Never!

- Cinnamon sticks. What a delicious smell. Place a bundle on your desk. Or put cinnamon sticks on your door in a wreath.

- Peppermint. Keep a dish of peppermint on your desk as a reward for your students or yourself.

- Branches of pine and fir. Pine and fir boughs, branches, and garlands. These fragrant trees can decorate your window sill; your reading center; your counter tops; anywhere. The greenery looks fresh and pretty alone. Or add natural cones, cones sprayed gold, artificial berries, silk or plastic poinsettias. Caution: Some people are allergic to fresh pine. Be alert to the needs of your class.

- Spray. Peruse the variety stores. Many fragrant sprays are available. Scents of trees, flowers, and spices are some popular ones. Test at home first and make sure you can tolerate the smell.

- Christmas Tree. Decorate a Christmas tree for the classroom, library, school office, or teachers' lounge. The tree will give cheerful warmth to the room. Real trees have a pleasant smell. For artificial ones, spray with fragrant sprays. Let children make decorations.

Art by Carol O'Regan.

CANDY CANE STICK HORSE ORNAMENT[149]

Gather Materials: Red felt; Cutout two horse head shapes for each ornament; Peppermint candy canes; Bead "eyes"; School glue; Black permanent marker

DIRECTIONS:

1. Make red felt horse heads (see illustration).

2. Give each child:
- A red felt horse head
- A peppermint cane
- An "eye"

3. Take turns using glue to:
- Glue two horse heads together. Glue only the top and bottom leaving ends open.
- Glue on "bead eye."

Peppermint stick horse ornament.

4. Take turns with black marker to draw a mouth. (Also draw the eyes with marker if you could not obtain bead eyes.)

5. Insert peppermint through mouth of horse.

Note: Let children take home ornament and hang by the cane holder.

GINGERBREAD

'Tis the season for eats, treats, rhythm, rhyme, and wonderful smells. Choose from these ideas with "Gingerbread":

- Read your favorite version of "The Gingerbread Man." See Illustration, page 141. Personally I like the versions that use the word MAN not BOY for the rhyme of "can" and "man" as in the nursery rhyme:

"Run, run as fast as you can
You can't catch me
I'm the gingerbread man."

- Buy bags of miniature cookies of gingerbread men or gingerbread bears.

- Bake a gingerbread cake in a bear shaped pan. Recite the rhyme "Teddy Bear" on page 96. The words: "Gin-ger-bread, Gingerbread turn around..." can be substituted for the words: "Ted-dy-bear, teddy bear."

- Enlist parent volunteers to assist you in baking one of the following:

- Make gingerbread squares.

- Make gingerbread cookies or gingerbread men.

- Make a large "Gingerbread Horn" for the class. Decorate with ABCs. See Chapter 3 for facts related to the Early American custom. Recite the rhyme on page 31.

"Gingerbread Man" by Carol O'Regan.

Ring Bells and Sing

Sing the song "Bells Are Ringing" on page 65. Give each child sleigh bells or jingle bells to shake as you sing.

Ring bells and sing before and after "Noel." Ring in the New Year using the song you learned before Christmas holidays, "Bells Are Ringing."

Help with rhythm. Directing or shaking bells, use a straight rhythm of 1, 2, 3, 4 for each line of the song. (Optional: You could shake a 1, 2, 3 rhythm on lines 3 and 4. But it would be better to continue to beat the four-rhythm for one count with no words. For example: "Child'-ren' sing x'," If you need help, ask the children — they will count the rhythm naturally!)

Jewish Holidays: Hanukkah Festival of Lights

There are many ancient Jewish holidays and each one has a special meaning. These holidays are based on the Hebrew calendar and some of the dates change from year to year.

Hanukkah means the festival or holiday of lights and is celebrated for eight days. Usually Hanukkah is celebrated in December. A special candleholder is used called a menorah. A menorah has a place for eight candles plus a candle in the center used to light all the others. During Hanukkah, Jewish families celebrate every night by lighting one more candle. On the eighth night all the candles are glowing, a special meal is eaten, songs are sung, and gifts are exchanged. Children spin a top called a dreidel and have fun playing a game.

Note: Be tolerant of other religions.

"Menorah" by Carol O'Regan.

Your school or public library has nonfiction books that clarify questions regarding Jewish holidays. Learn of their customs.[150] If there are children, who cannot participate in some of the class parties for religious reasons, speak to the principal and the librarian to see if they can be allowed to go to the library for recreational reading.

"ADreidel" by Carol O'Regan.

Winter Rhythms (January-February): Heart-Beats, Feed Birds, Arbor Day

Arbor Day and Tu Bishvat

Tu Bishvat or Tu B'Shebat is a holiday of trees celebrated in January or February. Jewish Arbor Day celebrates the planting of trees in Israel. The land of Israel is dry and thirsty. Some people send money to plant trees in Israel. If you have Jewish children, you can all celebrate the Holiday of Trees for it coincides with Arbor Day. For the holiday of trees, eat fruit and nuts that come from the types of trees and bushes grown in Israel: orange; carob; almond; olive.

Trees provide beauty, shade, shelter, and some food. Trees help purify our air and are important to everyone.

- Plant a tree.
- Read the lovely book *A Tree Is Nice* (Harper and Row, 1956) by Janice May Udry. The pictures by Marc Simont won the Caldecott Award. Mrs. Udry grew up around elm trees and planted an Ombu tree at her home.

According to Mrs. Udry, "In Spain the Ombu tree is called 'the tree of the beautiful shadow'. It grows to an immense size and is rarely found in America outside a botanical garden."

Winter Rhythms: January-February

- Trees and trains two "T's." Plant a tree. Read about trains.
- Trains. Read "The Engineer," the playful poem about a train, from *Now We Are Six* by A. A. Milne. Read *Freight Train*, the award-winning book by Donald Crews. Read straight through, showing the illustrations. Read again with a gentle rhythm, gently patting your knee or foot. Children pick up the rhythm. It's delightful. Read *Window Music* by Anastasia Suen and enjoy the rhythm of the sparse text and the colorful art by Zahares.
- President's Day. Two presidents have birthdays this month: Abraham Lincoln, February 12; and George Washington, February 22. In recent years they have been cel-

ebrated together and called "President's Day." You may choose to celebrate the birthdays separately.

- Hearts Activities. Valentine's Day is February 14. Are you having a class party? Enlist parent volunteers to plan games and refreshments. If your classes exchange valentines be sure to give one to every child in the class so each child will have at least one! See activities about hearts: cut-paper hearts, page 143; make a heart wreath, page 144; make torn-paper hearts, page 144; read Shel Silverstein's poem, "Love," page 125.

- Celebrate Black Heritage Month or Black History Month. Teach your students about black leaders they may not know.

- Leap Year. Is this year leap year? Some years February has 29 days!

- Stars. Have students look at the nighttime sky with someone in your family. Tell the class what you saw. Moon? Stars? Sing nursery rhyme "Twinkle-twinkle...star," page 64. Read *Watch the Stars Come Out* by Riki Levinson. Look at a picture of the beautiful state flag of Alaska. The field of blue of the Alaska state flag is a background for the gold stars of the Big Dipper and the North Star.

- Red Punch. Make a red punch for Valentine's or President's Day. Add red food coloring to "Basic Cold Punch" on page 156.

Cut Paper Hearts

How to cut paper hearts. Show children how to make a paper heart from any size piece of paper. (Note: Follow these directions for a right-handed child. Reverse for a left-handed teacher or child.[151])

1. Fold a piece of paper in half with the fold to the right.

2. With scissors, start cutting near the top, curving up to the top of the paper; then around to the outside and down to a point on the inside bottom right.

Note: You may want to lightly draw this step with pencil. With practice you can cut a heart free hand.

3. Open the paper and you will have a full heart shape.

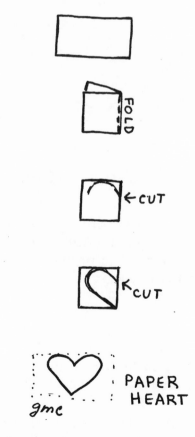

Steps to cutting a paper heart freehand.

Torn Paper Heart[152]

Torn paper heart. Follow the above directions with one exception. Instead of cutting with scissors, use the fingers to tear a little bit of paper at a time. Your thumb and index finger on each hand basically serve as scissors. Paper tearing gives an unusual effect. This method will be too hard for preschoolers. You will know your children's abilities. Children who enjoy working with their hands and like paper objects might enjoy making this different heart. Casually make one in front of the class (practice at home). Watch the children to discover interest. Give them a choice.

"Torn Heart" by author.

Make a Heart Wreath

Materials:

Heavy poster-board; colored construction paper; assorted gift wrapping paper; yarn string; ribbon (optional); scissors, and glue.

Preparation:

- On heavy poster-board draw a double circle.
- Cut out the center of the poster circles and cut the outer circle forming a ring.
- From colored paper or gift wrap, cut out many hearts of various sizes. (See "Cut Paper Hearts" if needed on age 143.)

- Note: Teachers or parents will need to complete the above preparation for very young preschoolers.

The Heart Wreath:

- Cover the ring with the hearts, overlapping some.
- Let children arrange the way they decide looks best.
- Glue the hearts to the ring.
- Add a yarn string to the top for hanging.
- Words may be added.
- Add ribbon or bows. (Optional.)

Variations:

The Heart Wreath may be used in a display; on a poster of contrasting color; bulletin board; door; or wall. Use anytime a love theme is appropriate. Suggestions: Christmas; the month of February; Valentine's Day; Mother's Day; Father's Day; or make in red, white and blue for a patriotic emphasis.

"Heart Wreath" by author.

Spring Rhythms (March-April-May): Feed Birds National Library Week Easter-Passover Field Trips

Spring: March, April, May Activities

- Spring holidays, Easter break, and parent-teacher conferences are all usually held in the Spring. Easter may be in April or May some years depending on the Spring Equinox. Schedule carefully these last months of the school year.

- Fairy Tales. Plan a Spring emphasis on folk tales and fairy tales. Read stories from the Brothers Grimm in Germany; Charles Perrault in France; and Hans Christian Andersen in The Netherlands. Many call some of Jane Yolen's books modern fairy tales. My favorites of her over 100 titles are *The Seeing Stick; Greyling;* and *Sleeping Ugly.*

- Feature materials from the National Wildlife Federation for March National Wildlife Week.

- Celebrate Hans Christian Andersen's birthday April 2. Read the autobiographical tale of "The Ugly Duckling."

- Booker T. Washington, American educator, was born April 5, 1856.

- Our third president, Thomas Jefferson (1743–1826), author and statesman, was born in Virginia on April 13, 1743. The Thomas Jefferson Building in Washington, called the Book Palace of the American People, has been restored.

  > "I cannot live without books!"
  > — Thomas Jefferson

- April 26 is the birthday of John James Audubon (1785–1851) the famous American ornithologist, naturalist, and artist. Spring is a fine time to study birds, watch birds and take the children on a nature walk. Listen to recordings of bird songs. Buy a classroom clock with bird songs on each hour.

- Feed Birds. A humorous bird feeding hint:

  "Instead of strewing seed about, pour about a cup of seed along a line about three feet long. Since nobody can plop in and hog it all, fighting is greatly diminished. The regulars line up on either side, just like well-behaved kids at a party."[153]

  The above feeding tip without the humor: On an imaginary line about three feet long, pour one cup of birdseed. The birds will eat from either side of the line.

- Learn to imitate bird songs.

- Participate in "Project Feeder Watch."[154]

- View a computer web site dedicated to birds! There's a bird of the week and a bird sound of the week. See http:birds.cornell.edu.

- Celebrate National Library Week in April. Order posters, bookmarks, and other materials from the American Library Association. Address is on page 158.

- May is Music Month. Sing "How I Love to Sing," page 70.

- Do not miss reading *The Carrot Seed* to pre-schoolers. This classic Spring story of planting and waiting was written by Ruth Krauss and illustrated by her husband, Crockett Johnson (Harper and Row, 1945). Some children can be patient, determined and hopeful, as is the child who planted "The Carrot Seed." Let children use their crayons to draw pictures of the story or of carrots to take home. The title is still in print and is in a sturdy board-edition. The children will ask you to re-read this story. Check with the cafeteria staff for menus when carrots will be served. Re-read the story before lunch. Children will enjoy the bright orange veggies. For a spring display include a colorful bunch of raw carrots with their lacy green tops. You may choose to serve carrots in class for a springtime treat. Carrot snack suggestions on page 155.

- Are you dreaming of spring? Perhaps it's March and one day you have sunshine and a hint of spring in the air. Then the next day the children are building snowmen at recess. Here's a book for you with several short stories to be read in late winter while you're hoping for spring. Or read at the first sign of spring. Enjoy the enchanting book *Waiting-for-Spring Stories* by Bethany Roberts with illustrations by Louisiana artist William Joyce. Seven little stories about rabbits are short enough for the shortest attention span. Suggestions: Read the stories one at the time to preschoolers. Read one or two stories a day for a week. Or read the entire book.

- The repetition and rhyme of *Over in the Meadow* by Olive Wadsworth can be enjoyed by showing children the lovely illustrations by Ezra Jack Keats as you read the words.

- For a Spring storytime for preschool through grades 2, read these books together: *Let's Make Rabbits* by Leo Lionni; *The Carrot Seed* by Ruth Krauss; and *What Is It?* by Tanya Hoban.

- Read *The Tale of Peter Rabbit* and *The Tale of Benjamin Bunny* (Peter's cousin) in springtime. Hold a toy stuffed rabbit under your arm as you read. Tell your second and third graders about the other classic books by Beatrix Potter.

- Sheep? Do you or your pupils know much about sheep or shearing? Probably not unless they live on a sheep farm in New England. Look in your library for the informative book *Spring Fleece*, sub-titled *A Day of Sheepshearing*. Catherine Paladino tells in prose and black-and-white photographs the story of shearing sheep in this excellent non-fiction book. Read to the older children and let younger children enjoy the pictures. Repeat rhyme: "Baa, baa ... have you any Wool?" How much? See pages 10–11.

JEWISH PASSOVER AND CHRISTIAN EASTER

The celebration of Passover comes in the spring, March or April. Jewish families hold a ceremony in their homes, a seder. Traditionally the youngest child asks a question: "Why is this night different from all other nights?" Those gathered to celebrate answer the question. They read the story of the Passover from Hebrew scripture.

Christians celebrate Easter.

Most schools have Spring holidays during this time.

Spring Field Trips

Read this humorous story before a field trip or just for fun.

Teachers who plan meaningful field trips also prepare the children for the experience. Thus a rewarding trip is insured for students, parent volunteers, and the teacher. In the dedication of her picture book titled *Lost in the Museum*,[155] Miriam Cohen wrote a thank-you note to the wonderful teachers who plan field trips for their students.

"For all the early childhood teachers who make school a place Jim likes to be."

— Miriam Cohen

The Story. Jim and his first grade schoolmates get *Lost in the Museum*. As part of the preparation before your next first grade field trip read this story by Miriam Cohen. Let the children enjoy the pictures by Lilian Hoban as you read. Children will get these messages loud and clear:

- Listen to the Teacher!

- "If we all stay together, nobody will get lost."

Summer Rhythms (June-July-August): Our Flag, Picnic Ice Cream, Watermelon Daydream

Many schools continue to meet into June making up "snow-days." Summer schools meet during these months. Some schools are operated year round. Use these suggested summer activities.

- Read books. The gifted illustrator Peter Spier was born in Amsterdam, The Netherlands, on June 6,

1927. Spier's books are colorful with lots of detail. Give children an opportunity to draw or paint after viewing Spier's work.

- June 14 is National Flag Day! Fly the American flag. In 1777 the "Stars and Stripes" became our national flag. Teach and model

"Sunflowers" by Carol O'Regan.

respect for the flag. Today salute the flag, honor the flag, and sing the national anthem.

- School-wide dress in red, white, and blue for the day.

- Make a flag cake. See directions in Appendix A, page 156.

- Celebrate the distinctly American holiday. Independence Day, our 4th of July.
  Riddle: Is there a 4th of July in Paris, France?
  Think about it: Of course the date, July 4 occurs everywhere.

    - Plan an outdoor picnic the day before your school holiday for July 4, our American Independence Day. Provide bag lunches, red nap-

kins, and small American flags. Watermelon for dessert.

- If you are in school these hot months, do celebrate July 23 by having ice cream! The ice cream cone was invented in 1904. You will need ice cream, cones or cups, napkins, and ice water.

- Celebrate the August 1 birthday of Francis Scott Key (1779), author of "The Star Spangled Banner."

- Play the beautiful music of the sea, "La Mer" by French composer Claude Debussy (1862–1918) on his birthday, August 22, or on another day during the month. See page 85.

- Daydream and dream dreams! Plan a place and a day to take your class to watch white fluffy clouds in a blue sky. Have each child bring a towel or mat. The day needs to be "just right, not too hot and not too cold." Take Peter Spier's book, *Dreams*, the class, and their mats. The last page has text in the almost wordless picture book. Show the book to children, turning the pages slowly, so they can see the colorful imaginative artwork by Peter Spier. After children have viewed the surprises in the book, have them spread out on their mats, look at the sky and find shapes in the clouds. Encourage the children to use their imaginations, gaze at the sky, and pretend the clouds are various shapes. Encourage conversation. After awhile go inside and let them draw what they saw while dreaming in the clouds.

Appendix A
Snacks and Recipes

Snacks

Caution! Food Alert! If you plan to serve any foods in your classroom during the school year you will want to send a form to parents at the beginning of the school year to ask if the children have any food allergies.

Some children are allergic to milk, cheese and milk products, tomatoes, seafood, shrimp, strawberries, nuts.

Important: Always wash your hands and have children always wash their hands before preparing or eating food!

1. Pretzels, Peanuts, and Punch. For a quick snack, combine pretzels and peanuts and serve with fruit punch.

2. Orange Smiles. Slice oranges into wedges forming "orange smiles!"

3. Cucumber Flowers. Make curly cucumber flowers in this way: Peel the cucumber. Then run the tines of a fork down the sides of the cucumber. Slice with a sharp knife. The slices will be curly. Several variations for curly cucumber slices:

- Eat crunchy curly cucumber slices.

- Make cucumber sandwiches. Spread cream cheese on bread slices. Cut in triangles. Place a curly cucumber on each triangle.

- Cut out bread in shapes using cookie cutters. Spread with cream cheese. Place a curly cucumber on the top. Hint: A cucumber fits nicely on a flower-shaped piece of bread.

4. Pineapple Butterflies. Make pretty butterflies like this: Use canned pineapple slices. Cut each slice in half and place the outside edges touching on the inside forming "butterfly wings." Garnish with olive slices on the top and bottom of each slice to form wing decorations. Place two strips of green or red bell pepper at the top to form the butterfly antennae.

"Pineapple Butterfly."

5. Peanut Butter Logs. Children can make this easy non-cook candy. See recipe, page 154.

6. Apples. Slice apples for a delicious healthy snack. Apples contain vitamins and minerals plus needed dietary fiber. When teaching the letter "A" show children a variety of apples, not just red ones. Apples can be golden yellow, spring green, or several shades of red. Introduce children to the names of various apples. They will remember if they're ready for the information. Ask grocery stores for large display pictures of apples and other fruit.

Prepare apples in the following manner:

- Wash each apple.

- Hold the apple firmly and press an apple corer through the center to remove core. Or carefully use a sharp knife. *Do not allow children to use sharp knives.*

- Slice the apple into wedges.

- Use a paring knife or melon baller to remove center and carefully cut out seeds (seeds are poisonous).

- Eat apple immediately or sprinkle slices with lemon juice and place in water to prevent discoloring.

7. **Peel a Banana**! My daughter returned from a visit to Belize with a trick for peeling a banana. Try the fun method. It works.

- Turn the banana to the opposite end you usually peel.

- Pinch and pull the brown point on the end of the banana.

- Peel and eat. This delicious fruit is loaded with healthy potassium.

Suggestions: Teaching the letter "B" to nursery and kindergarten children, serve bananas as a healthy snack. Divide the children in groups of two to each eat half of a banana. A whole banana may be too much for small stomachs.

For fun, read a story about an ape, monkey or gorilla and let the children have a healthy snack of bananas. Show them this trick. Let them choose whether or not to try the different way of peeling a banana.

8. **Make and Eat Artichoke Balls**. Older children can make artichoke balls. There may be too many "messy" steps for younger children although they will enjoy eating this dish. See recipe, page 155.

9. **Prepare Soft Carrots**. Serve carrots in springtime, when reading stories about rabbits, or anytime as a healthy snack. See the recipe on page 155.

10. **Frozen Fruit on a Stick**. For a healthy snack serve frozen fruit. Freeze the whole fruit, cut into pieces; or add a stick. I especially like frozen whole seedless green grapes.

11. **Frozen Fruit Sorbet**. For a delicious treat ask a parent volunteer to make frozen fruit sorbet for your class. See the recipe "Fresh Fruit Sorbet" on page 156.

12. **Edible Play Dough**. What fun making and eating play dough! Optional decoration: raisins. See recipe for "Bee's Edible Play Dough" on page 153.

13. **Foods with Protein**. Sometimes school class parties can provide food children need. Foods rich in protein are peanut butter; nuts; cheese; and tuna fish. Parents groups may help provide these foods.

Specific Suggestions: peanut butter fudge; peanut butter play dough; paper cups of nuts for each child; cheese sandwiches; tuna sandwiches; provide cookie cutters for children to cut-out seasonal shapes from cheese slices.

14. **Eat the Alphabet.** Sometimes snacks can correlate with "the letter of the day" in classes for younger children. Consider: Animal cookies; Artichoke (page 155); Apple (page 150); Banana (page 150); Beans (page 151); Bell-Pepper (page 151); Carrot (page 155); Celery; Cheese; Cookies (page 152); Corn; Cucumber (page 149); Fruit; Fudge (page 154); Gingerbread (page 141); Ice Cream; Juice; Lettuce; Milk; Nuts; Orange (page 149); Peanut; Peach; Pear; Pineapple (page 149); Plum; Popcorn (page 59); Potato; Pretzel (page 149); Pumpkin; Tomato; Zest (page 114) and others.

15. **Eat Veggies.** Prepare fresh vegetables attractively for healthy snacks. Wash, prepare and refrigerate until serving. Make these: cucumber sticks; sliced cucumbers with peel; sliced curly cucumbers (page 149); small cherry tomatoes (bite size, or cut in half); carrot sticks; carrot coins (recipe, Copper Pennies, page 155); celery sticks for younger children you may have to pull strings off); bell pepper circles; bell pepper sticks; yellow pepper slices.

Beans are a good source of protein. Combine three or four kinds of your favorite beans; place in a plastic container; marinate in Italian dressing; refrigerate until eating. Serve cold. Eating requires a small cup or plate and a spoon. Good for an end-of-school picnic.

16. **Pizza Trees.** Occasion: Make pizza trees for any occasion. Or for these special occasions: Christmas party; Arbor Day tree planting; celebrate Spring and the end of a long winter.

Directions: Make a pizza according to package directions. Cut away dough to make tree shape. Spread meat and sauce around "tree." Bake. Make a tree trunk with a piece of celery stalk or a strip of green bell pepper.

For "Christmas Tree": Use pepperoni, mushrooms, or black olives like tree decorations. Spread cheese as shown to make garlands. From yellow, red, or green sweet pepper cut a small star. Add trunk from celery. Tool needed: Small Star Cookie Cutter

"Piza Tree" by author.

17. **"Green Eggs and Ham."** If you are brave, bring an electric skillet and two dozen eggs to class. As a follow-up activity after reading Dr. Seuss' *Green Eggs and Ham*, cook green eggs for your class. Do you really want to do ham too? OK![156]

DIRECTIONS: Actually you'll need more than just the skillet and eggs. Think through your procedures; decide where you will cook in the classroom; gather supplies in a sturdy cardboard box from the grocery store; give the children some safety guidelines; read the story; cook the eggs; serve to the children.

GATHER MATERIALS: 2 dozen eggs; green food coloring; 1 pint of milk; fork and bowl for mixing; cooking oil, small amount; electric skillet; dish-towel; hot pad; paper plates and plastic forks for serving.

18. Healthy Snacks and Treats.

Yogurt Sundae: Serve frozen or regular yogurt in a plastic cup or dish. Add fresh fruit. Pour honey on the top. Sprinkle with granola or chopped nuts. Top with a maraschino cherry.

Easy Dessert: Serve small pieces of fruit with small separate bowls of sour cream and brown sugar. Let each child get a piece of fruit and dip the fruit first into the sour cream and then into the brown sugar.

Apple Custard: Preheat oven to 350°. Wash, peel, and core apple. Slice very thin. Sprinkle with brown sugar. Beat one egg. Fold into apples. Put into well-buttered baking dish. Bake for 30 minutes.

Orange Sherbet Cups: Let children work in pairs. Slice oranges in half. Scoop out pulp with a spoon. Eat pulp; fill cups with orange sherbet. Freeze. Eat another day. A double-treat.

Juice Popsicles: Freeze juice (apple, orange, white grape or cranberry) in small paper cups. Optional: Popsicle sticks or candy sticks may be inserted before completely frozen.

19. Cookies.

Plain cookies for schoolchildren include: shaped animal cookies, vanilla wafers, butter cookies, gingersnaps, and raisin biscuits.

Shaped Cookies: Make shaped cookies cut out in any shape to coordinate with a lesson, holiday theme, or schoolwide promotion. Look for these cookie cutters: bear; star, moon, tree, wreath, candy-cane, rabbit, turkey. You can also make simple shapes: circles, triangles, rectangles, squares. Or order and buy shaped cookies from a bakery. Ask bakery department if they will bake unusual shapes if you provide the cutters. Many will.

Cookie Recipes in This Book. "Cathy's Peanut Butter Logs" is an easy no-bake candy recipe you can make in class. Recipe, page 154. A "S'more" is a type of cookie. Instructions on page 154. A "Hot Cross Bun" could be like an English biscuit for teatime. Or use for a Doll or Teddy Bear Tea Party. See directions on page 21. Eat gingersnaps, gingerbread cookies, or gingerbread men. For suggestions look in Chapter 10 on page 141. The recipe for boiled cookies came from a university children's literature class. The teacher had us take turns bringing snacks. We decided such a delicious cookie needed a fancier name, thus: "Charlie-Brown Cookies" (see page 155).

Make Classroom Sweets. All these sweets can be made in your classroom:

- "Cathy's Peanut Butter Logs." No cooking, page 154.

- "Charlie Brown Cookies." Microwave needed, page 155.

- "Ginger's Fudge." Microwave needed, page 154.

20. Cookie Container.

For an unusual attractive container use cookie dough pressed around a foil-covered container (oven proof bowl or pan, any shape) and bake. The container will be edible. Fill the edible holder with cookies or candy for an unusual table decoration.

DIRECTIONS:

Cover the outside of an oven proof bowl or loaf pan with foil. Spray with vegetable cooking spray.

Preheat oven to 350° F.

Make your favorite cookie dough. Cut out circles of cookie dough. (Note: Use scalloped cutter if possible.)

Cover container with cookie dough cutouts, slightly overlapping them.

Bake about 10 to 12 minutes, until brown. Cool on wire rack. Carefully separate cookie container from foil.

Serve candy or cookies from the container.

Recipes

Bee's Edible Play Dough

INGREDIENTS:

18 ounces peanut butter

6 Tablespoons honey

non-fat dry milk (or milk plus flour to the right consistency)

DIRECTIONS: Have children wash hands thoroughly.

Mix ingredients. Shape and play with dough. Decorate with raisins and eat!

NOTES: An adult should measure the correct amounts. Allow children to combine the ingredients and play with the mixture. It's PLAY-Dough! After playing for awhile, decorate with raisins and eat!

CAUTION: The next time you give the children regular Play-doh, remember to remind them: "Do not eat, just play."

— Marianne Wheeler

Pudding Finger-Paint

INGREDIENTS:

Instant pudding mix

Waxed paper

Individual plastic trays

DIRECTIONS: Have children wash hands throughly. Make pudding by package directions. Give each child an individual plastic tray covered with waxed paper. Scoop about ½ cup of pudding onto waxed paper. Instruct each child to spread the pudding around with fingers and hands. Have fun painting with the thick "finger-paint." Tell the children, "Surprise. You are painting with pudding! You may lick your fingers and eat the rest!"

CLEAN UP: Have a plastic liner in your trashcan. Let children finish playing and eating. Help class dispose of the waxed paper. Stack trays in a designated place. Go to bathroom and wash hands with soap.

NOTE: Enlist help. Ask the kitchen staff if you can use the cafeteria trays at a time convenient to their meal schedules. Arrange to wash the trays. Enlist parent volunteers to help you with this project.

Apple Turkey

INGREDIENTS (PER CHILD):

One apple

11 or 12 toothpicks

Raisins

One olive

Pimento

DIRECTIONS: Let each child make an apple turkey as follows: Thread raisins onto toothpicks. Stick one raisin-filled toothpick in each side of the apple forming "wings." Place one "raisin stick" in the top forming a neck. Place an olive on the end of this toothpick forming a head. Place a piece of pimento hanging from the olive to form the turkey wattle. Place remaining "raisin toothpicks" in a fan shape across the back of the apple forming the tail feathers of the turkey. Use 5 to 7 depending on the size of the apple.

Children can take these home to use as table favors for Thanksgiving dinner.

"Apple Turkey" by Carol O'Regan.

S'mores

What is it? A sweet dessert that's so good everyone asks for *some more*—s'more! These are always part of our family camping menus. Children love them. For an unusual treat, make at school. When? Ideas: Western Day (Have a teacher supervise toasting marshmallows at an outdoor bonfire or a fire in a bar-b-que grill). Promise as a reward for good behavior. Or you can make s'mores in a portable microwave moved into class.

DIRECTIONS: Place a plain chocolate candy bar between two graham cracker halves. Roast a large marshmallow over coals until golden brown and place on chocolate. Press together like a sandwich and eat. Delicious. Have s'more!

MICROWAVE DIRECTIONS: Place the entire "sandwich" on a plain white paper towel in the microwave for 10 to 15 seconds.

Cathy's Christmas Candy

INGREDIENTS:
1 cup peanut butter, chunky

2 Tablespoons margarine
1¼ cups sifted powdered (confectioners') sugar
3 cups Rice Krispies cereal
chopped peanuts

DIRECTIONS: Blend peanut butter and margarine in a bowl. Stir in sugar. Add cereal, crushing slightly. Mix well. Shape into three logs. Pat peanuts over the logs of dough. Wrap in foil or clear plastic wrap. Chill in refrigerator.

Slice peanut butter logs into 1/2-inch thick slices.

Yield: One pound of candy.
— Cathy Caughman

Ginger's Microwave Fudge

INGREDIENTS:
12 ounces semi-sweet chocolate chips
12 ounces butterscotch chips
1 cup smooth peanut butter
1 cup graham crackers, crushed
1 cup chopped pecans
1 cup pecan halves
72 one-inch cupcake baking-cups (miniature size)

DIRECTIONS: Place chips and peanut butter into an 8-cup glass measuring cup. Microwave on medium high (70%) for five minutes. Stir until smooth. Add crumbs and chopped pecans. Mix well.

Drop by large teaspoons-full into cupcake liners. Decorate each top with a pecan half. Refrigerate 30 minutes to harden.

NOTES: A delicious candy recipe. Take a microwave into your room and make in class. Place in refrigerator in teachers' lounge, office lounge or kitchen. (Check with the kitchen staff a day ahead to make sure they will have room.)

UNO Charlie Brown Cookies (Boiled Cookies)

INGREDIENTS:
  1 cup sugar
  2 tablespoons cocoa
  ¼ cup milk
  ½ stick margarine
  ½ teaspoon vanilla
  ¼ cup crunchy peanut butter
  1¼ cups quick cooking oats

DIRECTIONS: Mix first 4 ingredients. Place over medium heat and boil for one minute. Remove from heat and add remaining ingredients. Mix well and drop by spoonfuls onto waxed paper. Cool until hardened. Enjoy!

— Colleen Salley

Artichoke Balls

Children will enjoy making and eating this simple delicious dish. For many it will be their first time to eat artichoke. Ask, "Who has eaten an artichoke?" "What is an artichoke?" Show a picture obtained from the grocery, print a picture from the Internet, or try to obtain at least one fresh artichoke to show the source of the delicious artichoke heart.

INGREDIENTS:
  2 cans artichoke hearts, drained
  1 large garlic clove, put through press (optional)
  ½ cup grated Parmesan cheese
  ½ cup seasoned Italian breadcrumbs
  2 to 4 tablespoons olive oil
  Salt and white pepper to taste (white pepper is easier to digest than black pepper)

PREPARATION:
- Wash hands!
- Preheat oven to 350-degrees.
- Lightly grease cookie sheet.

DIRECTIONS:
- **Artichokes:** Drain and cut artichokes in half. Squeeze to remove juice and form into a sort of lumpy "ball."
- **Crumb mixture:** Combine bread crumbs, Parmesan cheese, salt and pepper.
- **Oil:** In a separate dish place a small amount of olive oil. Optional: Add garlic if desired.
- **Make Balls:** Make balls as follows: Alternately roll artichoke in oil then in bread crumb mixture. With hands form a ball of crumbs around the pieces of artichoke. Roll in more cheese if desired. Place balls on lightly greased cookie sheet. Refrigerate until time to cook.
- **Cook:** Heat in microwave or oven. Microwave until heated through or bake in 350-degree oven for 15 minutes.
- **To Make Ahead:** After shaping mixture into balls, freeze on cookie sheet. After frozen, transfer to zipper freezer bags. When ready to serve, place frozen balls on lightly greased cookie sheet and bake in 350-degree oven for 20 minutes or until golden brown.

— Ginger Caughman

Ginger's Copper Pennies

Carrots are such a beautiful color. I like the name for this recipe, "Copper Pennies." The marinated carrots can be prepared at home and brought to school in a wide mouth jar. Refrigerate until serving. Provide children plastic forks and a decorated fall or spring napkin.

INGREDIENTS:

  5 cups sliced fresh carrots
  1 medium onion, sliced
  1 medium green pepper, sliced
  ½ cup Crisco oil
  ¾ cup vinegar
  1 can Campbell's tomato soup
  1 cup granulated sugar
  1 teaspoon pepper
  1 teaspoon dry mustard
  1 teaspoon Lea & Perrins sauce

DIRECTIONS: Boil carrots in salted water until tender, about 5 minutes. Drain and place carrots in Pyrex or Corning-Ware dish. Add sliced onion and green pepper and set aside.

In a separate pot mix remaining ingredients and bring to a boil. Pour hot mixture over vegetables.

Place in covered container. Refrigerate overnight for flavors to mingle. Keeps for weeks in the refrigerator.

— Mildred Barlow Caughman

Fresh Fruit Sorbet

INGREDIENTS:

  1 banana, peeled and cut into thirds
  ¾ cup fresh or frozen peaches or strawberries
  2 Tablespoons honey

DIRECTIONS: Place each kind of fruit in a separate freezer bag. Freeze fruit for four to six hours. Remove bags from freezer about 20 minutes before use.

Place banana in food processor fitted with metal blade. Pulse on and off until fruit is smooth. Add peaches (or other fruit) and puree until thick. Do not over-puree. Place in parfait or sherbet glasses or glass bowls. Refrigerate or freeze until ready to serve.

NOTES: This recipe yields two servings. Adjust amount of fruit to make sorbet for an entire class. Vary fruit if desired.

Nell's Flag Cake

INGREDIENTS:

  One box yellow or white cake mix
  Rectangle baking pan (12" × 8")
  1 whipped topping (8 oz.)
  ⅓ cup blueberries
  3 cups strawberry halves, sliced

DIRECTIONS: Make cake by package directions, baking in rectangle pan. Cool.

Cover top of cake with whipped topping. Arrange a small corner of blueberries on the top left corner of the cake. This will be your field of stars. Arrange strawberry slices in rows across the cake to look like stripes on the flag.

Refrigerate till serving.

— Nell Rose Gill Morris

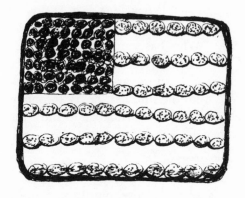

"Flag Cake" by Carol O'Regan.

Lynn's Basic Cold Punch

To make a basic punch, combine and freeze:

  4 cups water
  42 ounces pineapple juice
  2 cups sugar
  12 ounces frozen orange juice
  6 ounces frozen lemonade

Take frozen mixture above and add Sprite, 7-Up, or ginger ale. (Choose your favorite.)

SERVING IDEAS: A basic cold punch recipe has many uses. Try all of these suggestions: Serve the "Basic Punch" cold. Freeze "Basic Punch" and serve in paper cups as sherbet, slush, or snow cone. Place frozen "Basic Punch" into a large container or punchbowl and pour a clear beverage over the frozen punch (this keeps punch cool without diluting).

Basic Cold Punch #2

INGREDIENTS:

Same as for "Basic Cold Punch," above, plus 6 bananas.

DIRECTIONS: Into a blender place water, sliced bananas, and sugar. Blend to liquid stage.

Pour half of mixture into large plastic bowl (approximately 10" across). In blender with other half of mixture, add lemonade and orange juice. Mix.

Pour contents of blender plus pineapple juice into the plastic bowl. Stir and mix well. Pour into punch bowl and serve, adding clear beverage; or freeze.

SERVING IDEAS: Serve frozen or partially thawed as a sherbet, slush, or snow cone. Or pour lemon-lime drink over as a punch.

Enjoy this delicious recipe in any of its variations.

— Lynn B. Thorne
Raleigh, North Carolina

Elsie's Hot Fruit Punch

INGREDIENTS:

3 quarts water

1½ cups granulated sugar
1 large 46-oz. can orange juice
Juice of 3 lemons
2 cups pineapple juice
1 or 2 cinnamon sticks

DIRECTIONS: Combine above ingredients in a large boiler. Slice two fresh oranges and float in the punch. Squeeze some of the fresh juice into the punch. Put on high heat but do not boil! Serve hot. Delicious.

NOTE: Can be stored in the refrigerator in a covered container and reheated one cup at a time.

— Elsie Ballard Egger
Columbus, Mississippi

Children like the basic cold punch and the hot fruit punch. Save the spiced percolator punch below for parent or faculty gatherings.

Hot Spiced Percolator Punch

Combine these ingredients in a 30 cup coffee urn:
9 cups unsweetened pineapple juice
9 cups cranberry juice cocktail
4½ cups water
1 cup brown sugar

Place the following in the percolator basket:
4½ teaspoons whole cloves
4 cinnamon sticks, broken
½ teaspoon salt

Plug in and perk! Serve hot.

— Maudellen Welch
Ft. Walton Beach, Florida

Appendix B
Resources and Addresses

On Sitting Still
Muriel F. Blackwell

He told me just to sit right here,
But not to make a sound;
And he would teach me all the truths
Within the lessons found.
Although I sat still on the chair,
My mind went out to play;
For God's blue sky called out to me,
"This is a lovely day."
I soared the vast expanse of space
Without an earthly care,
And built me castles in the clouds,
Yet never left that chair.
It's true I didn't make a sound;
But he could not discern,
That sitting still does not assure
A single thing I'll learn!

© Muriel F. Blackwell
Used by permission

Addresses

American Foundation for the Blind
15 West 16th Street
New York, New York 10011

American Library Association (ALA)
50 East Huron Street
Chicago, Illinois 60611-2795
Phone: 1-800-545-2433

Fax: 312-944-8520
Email: *www./ala.org*

The American Library Association's "Randolph Caldecott Medal" is given annually for the best picture book in American children's literature published the previous year.

Randolph Caldecott was a nineteenth century English illustrator. To encourage American artists to produce excellent picture books for children, the American Library Association began awarding the Randolph Caldecott Medal in 1938 for the best American picture book for children published the previous year. Thus the gold seal of "The Caldecott Medal" on the cover of a book indicates an excellence of art and illustration.

You may not like the story of every Caldecott winner, but do view and appreciate the artwork. Look at all of the books in this tradition of over sixty years. You'll also want to view those books designated the "Caldecott Honor Books." Each year one or more books are selected as the runner-up. Find books you especially like and read those favorites to children.

The American Toy Institute, Inc. (ATI)
Affiliated with Toy Manufactures of
America, Inc. (TMA)

1115 Broadway–Suite 400
New York, New York 10010
Phone: 1-212-675-1141
Website: *www.toy-tma.org*

See also:

- Toy Safety information see U.S. Consumer Safety which includes TOYS (CPSC). To report a hazardous product contact CPSC at 1-800-638-2722.
- National Lekotek Center for Toys for Children with Disabilities.
- ATI works with American Foundation for the Blind to produce brochure, *Guide to Toys for Children Who Are Blind or Visually Impaired*. Write for free copies.

Audubon Society
National Audubon Society
Membership Department/FW
700 Broadway
New York, New York 1003
Telephone: 1-800-274-4201
E-mail: *join@audubon.org*
http://www.audubon.org/

The Classroom Feeder Watch is a joint project of the National Audubon Society and the Cornell Laboratory of Ornithology. (*See* **Cornell Laboratory of Ornithology**.)

Binney and Smith, Inc.
1100 Church Lane
P.O. Box 431
Easton, PA 18044-0431
Phone: 1-800-CRAYOLA
1-800-272-9652
Email: *www.crayola.com*

"Crayola crayons were invented by Binney & Smith in 1902. Mrs. Binney coined the trade name 'Crayola' from French words 'craie' (stick of color) and 'ola' (oily)."[157] Today there are 120 different crayons. An exact recipe is followed so the colors are always the same.[158] The word "Crayola" in this book is used by permission.[159]

The Caldecott Award *see* **American Library Association**

Center for the Book *see* **The Library of Congress**

The Children's Book Council, Inc.
568 Broadway–Suite 404
New York, New York 10012
Phone: 1-212-966-1990
Phone: 1-800-999-2160
Fax: 212-966-2073
Email: *staff@cbcbooks.org*
Online: *www.cbcbooks.org*

Cobblestone Publishing
7 School Street
Peterborough, NH 03458
Phone: 1-800-821-0115

Cobblestone publishes seven excellent magazines (on shiny paper). Magazines feature geography, U.S. history, world history, and different cultures. Theme Issues. The magazine appropriate for young children (especially grades 2-4) is *Appleseeds*, each issue featuring general and United States history, geography, and science. Call for a free sample.

Cornell Laboratory of Ornithology
159 Sapsucker Woods Road
Ithaca, New York 14850

The Cornell Laboratory of Ornithology is a membership institute dedicated to the study, appreciation, and conservation of birds worldwide. The citizen-science projects include:

- Cornell Nest Box Network
- Project Feeder Watch

- Birds in Forested Landscapes
- Project Pigeon Watch
- House Finch Disease Survey
- Classroom Feeder Watch
- Bird of the Week
- Sound of the Week.

Phone: 1-607-254-2482
1-800-843-BIRD
Email: *http:birdsource.cornell.edu*
Homepage: *http/birds.cornell.edu*

"Crayola" *see* **Binney and Smith, Inc.**

Gallaudet University and
Gallaudet University Press
800 Florida Avenue, NE
Washington, DC 20002-3695
Phone: 1-202-651-5488

Highsmith Inc.
P. O. Box 800
Ft. Atkinson, WI 53538-0800
Phone: 1-800-558-2110
Website: *www.highsmith.com*

Offers catalog of school and library supplies. Call for free catalog of materials for teachers of younger children including posters, bookmarks, banners, stickers, and other promotional materials.

The Horn Book, Inc.
The Horn Book Magazine
56 Roland Street — Suite 200
Boston, MA 02129
Phone: 1-800-325-1170
Phone: 1-617-628-0225
Hours: M-F, 9-5 EST
FAX: 617-628-0885
HomePage: *www.hb.com*

More about the "Horn Books." The Horn-books were bound on the edges by brass strips. "Most of the horn-books were two and ¾ inches by five inches."

"The Horn Book"
by author.

The sheets of vellum or parchment held lessons. The content? the alphabet, large and small letters, vowels and consonants, and "The Lord's Prayer." The purpose? In general to teach children their "letters" and to continue religious instruction.[160]

The Horn Book Magazine was named for the early American so-called horn-books. The magazine is an excellent resource for librarians, teachers, and parents. An enjoyable periodical to read about new books and the world of children's literature, *The Horn-Book Magazine* is published six times a year. The standards and literary quality are high. Book reviews and illustrations are printed. The summer issue annually publishes the acceptance speeches of the American Library Association's Caldecott and Newbery winners.

Ideal/Instructional Fair Publishing Group

(Division of Tribune Education)
Call toll-free switchboard for catalogs or information:

- **Instructional Fair-TS Denison**
- **Ideal-Instructional Fair Publication**

P.O. Box 3241
Grand Rapids, MI 49501
Toll free call: 1-800-443-2976 or
Telephone: 1-800-253-5469
E-mail: *http://www.instructionalfair.com*

"Instructional Fair-TS Denison" produces "Shape Seals" in these designs: apples; bears; circus; musical instruments; space vehicles; dinosaurs; zoo animals; insects; ocean; rainforest animals; butterflies; reptiles; farm animals; 50 states; hearts; neon space; neon sports; neon tropical fish; gold foil and multicolored foil stars; dollars; solar system; U.S. flag; and wild west.

International Reading Association

800 Barksdale Road
P. O. Box 8139
Newark, Delaware 19714-8139

The Library of Congress Center for the Book

Director: John Y. Cole
101 Independence Avenue, S.E.
Washington, DC 20540-4920

- NATIONAL: John Y. Cole has been director of "The Library of Congress Center for the Book" since it was established in 1977. The purpose was to stimulate public interest in books and reading and to encourage the study of books and reading as forces in the shaping of society. Private and corporation contributions support the symposia, lectures, projects, and publications.

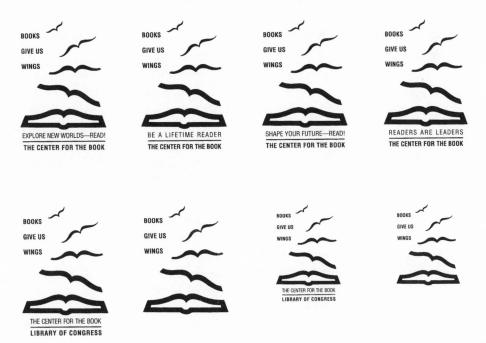

"Books Give Us Wings," used by permission, The Center for the Book.

- STATE: Statewide affiliates of the Center for the Book extend its mission to the state and local level and are now located in 36 states.
- LOGOS: The Center for the Book has given permission for you to reprint the logos or adapt them for your use. See pages 93, 97, 161.

National Geographic Society
P.O. Box 2118
Washington, DC 20013-2118
Phone: 1-800-368-2728
Educational-Customer Service

High quality materials. Write or call for a catalog of information.

National Poison Control Center
A number is available nationally and staffed 24 hours a day around the United States. Most states have their own number. In the West some states are combined into areas. You can easily find the number for your state or area. Look in the front of your phone book with other emergency numbers.

Emergency information you need when calling:

- What is the condition of the child now?
- What are the child's symptoms?
- What is the age and weight of the child? (Approximate if not known.)
- What was the poison? How much poison was ingested?
- What is the phone number and address of the nearest hospital?

Notewell's Book Darts
3945 Willow Flat Road
Hood River, Oregon 97031
1-800-366-2230

Fax: 541-354-3949
E-mail: *bookdarts@aol.com*

Teachers, mark your favorite passages in your personal books with these small metal tabs. "Book Darts" will become your favorite bookmarks.

"Nota bene" is Latin for "note well," thus the name "Notewell's Book Darts." Designed and classroom tested by a high school teacher, the metal "Book Darts" are archival quality lightweight pointers made of bronze. Unlike a paper clip these markers will not damage your books or papers. Produced by Bob and Jeanette Williams. Keep away from children, as the small metal pieces could be a hazard. *Not for young children!* For teachers, librarians, educators and all adults.

Prevent Blindness America
500 East Remington Road
Schaumburg, Illinois 60173-5611
Phone: 1-800-331-2020
Fax: 847-843-8458

United States Consumer Product Safety Commission (CPSC)
An independent, federal regulatory agency that protects the public against unreasonable risks and injury associated with consumer products, including toys.

To report a hazardous product or injury contact the CPSC at 1-800-638-2772. The CPSC website is: *www.cpsc.gov*

Upstart
(A Division of Freline, Inc.)
Box 889
Hagerstown, Maryland 21741
Phone# 1-800-448-4887
Fax# 1-301-797-1615

Promotion materials. Order catalog or place an order. Hours: 7 A.M.-7 P.M. CST, M–F.

Weston-Woods
(Subsidiary of Scholastic)
12 Oakwood Avenue
Norwalk, CT 06850-1318
Call toll free: 1-800-243-5020

Order high quality videos and books with read-along cassettes.

Founder Morton Schindel began adapting children's picture books to film in 1953. His purpose is to create multimedia adaptations that are faithful reflections of the original books and preserve the integrity of the original. Weston Woods uses three criteria for book selection for adaptations: desirability, adaptability, and availability. In 1998, Weston-Woods merged with Scholastic. Excellent material.

Notes

Introduction

1. *Webster's New World Dictionary of the American Language*, 2nd College Edition. N.Y.: Simon and Schuster (Gulf and Western Corporation). My own *Webster's* dictionary was used as a reference tool for this book. Quotation marks are used when quoted directly. Here the use of the words "rhythm" and "rhyme" are selected and adapted to the purposes of this book.

2. Arbuthnot, May. *Children and Books*, rev. ed. Chicago: Scott, Foresman, 1957, p. 195 (used by permission). This book, my college text at MSCW, taught by Mrs. Alice James Gatchell, was my introduction to the wonderful world of children's literature and is used as a reference in this book. The stunning phrase "contagious rhythms" is a graphic one for this book on teaching with rhythm and rhyme. In its context, Arbuthnot was writing about Mother Goose as a natural starting point in "Using Poetry with Children," her Chapter 9. The exact quote is: "They [children] don't know that it is meter and rhyme, line and word patterns that produce these contagious rhythms, but they feel the 'going-ness' of the verses."

3. Blackwell, Muriel. The poem "On Sitting Still" conveys a poignant truth. Muriel F. Blackwell has graciously granted permission for the poem to be reproduced from the out-of-print title *Potter and Clay*. (Broadman Press, 1975). The copyright has reverted back to Blackwell. See Appendix B, p. 158 for the poem.

4. Trueblood, Elton. A favorite phrase of the master teacher. The direct reference is to Dr. Rendel Harris, teacher at Johns Hopkins University. Trueblood wrote of Harris: "He came to illustrate for me what I later began to call the clear head and the warm heart." *The Teacher*, D. Elton Trueblood, Broadman Press, Nashville, Tennessee, 1980, p. 16. Trueblood often said: "Teachers need a clear head and a warm heart."

Chapter 1: Mother Goose Rhymes

5. Arbuthnot, *op. cit*, p. 57.

6. *Webster's* dictionary.

7. Arbuthnot, *op. cit.*, p. 43.

8. Allemands Elementary School, Des Allemands (St. Charles Parish), Louisiana.

9. *The World Book Encyclopedia*, vol. 14, "N," p. 457.

10. Many claim to be *the* Mary. *Bartlett's Familiar Quotations*, John Bartlett (Boston: Little, Brown, 1980), p. 463, credits Mary Elizabeth Sawyer of Sterling, Massachusetts.

11. *Mother Goose*: The Volland Edition. Re-arranged and edited by Eulalie Osgood Grover. Illustrated by Frederick Richardson. Chicago: M. A. Donohue, 1915. I still have this edition of Mother Goose given to me when I was three by my Mother's friend, Frances Merle Reid.

12. Many claim authorship of the nursery rhyme, "Mary Had a Little Lamb." *World Book* states that Sara Hale wrote the verses

(*World Book, op. cit.,* volume H, p. 19) but *Bartlett's* disagrees. John Bartlett credits John Roulstone the author of the first three stanzas and Sara Hale the last three. A fascinating history of the poem, "The Story of Mary's Little Lamb" (1928), was published by Mr. and Mrs. Henry Ford and is summarized in *Bartlett's. op. cit.,* p. 463. The Fords insist "the events of the poem are true."

13. Tomie de Paola's research for his illustrations in *Mary Had a Little Lamb,* Holiday House (1984), conclude that Sarah Josepha Burell Hale was the sole author of the poem "Mary's Lamb." Like the "Mother Goose controversy" there are many opinions. Whatever you choose to believe about the disagreement I believe that you will enjoy de Paola's charming illustrations in his recognizable style. The reference to the poem's authorship at the end of his book is interesting, as is the information about Sarah Hale in the beginning of the book. De Paola's buildings in his illustrations are based on architecture near his home in New Hampshire.

14. *Ring a Ring o'Roses: Stories, Games, and Finger Plays for Pre-School Children.* From the Flint Public Library, Flint, Michigan, p. 88. Permission to quote from supervisor, Cynthia Stilley.

Chapter 2: Activities with Mother Goose Rhymes

15. In childhood, Saturday mornings for me were waiting for the radio show *Let's Pretend.* Help children express creativity and develop imagination by telling original stories from their lives and listening to you tell and read stories. For more on the radio show see: *Let's Pretend: A History of Radio's Best Loved Children's Show by a Longtime Cast Member.* Arthur Anderson. McFarland, 1994.

16. "The name Mother Goose has now become so completely associated with the popular verses that most English transla-tions of the Perrault tales omit it from the title of the stories." Arbuthnot, *op. cit.,* p. 57.

17. For several years I taught workshops for children's teachers. A filmstrip I showed over and over had a phrase I'd experienced in my teaching and always emphasized to teachers: "Beware lest the production become an end in itself."

18. Have your dictionary on your desk and let the children see you using it as often as needed. "Nimble" can refer to mental or physical agility. "Mentally quick and alert; moving or acting quickly or alertly," as when Joan or Jack jumped over the candlestick. These rhymes are in Chapter 1.

19. Charlotte is a spider, the star of E. B. White's classic children's story, *Charlotte's Web.*

20. See Appendix B for Resources and Addresses for promotional materials for Children's Book Week. Use ideas from this book. Write, email, or call these organizations for assistance with special materials prepared annually: American Library Association, the Children's Book Council, or Upstart. See ideas also for National Library Week held annually in April.

21. Arbuthnot, *op. cit.,* pp. 74–75.

22. Arbuthnot, *Ibid.*

23. Arbuthnot, *op. cit.,* p. 75.

Chapter 3: Move with Rhyme and Rhythm

24. Sloane, Eric. I found this old rhyme in Eric Sloane's delightful book, *ABC Book of Early Americana: A Sketchbook of Antiquities and American Firsts,* New York: Wings Books, 1963. Published 1995 by Random House by arrangement with Henry Holt, © 1963 by Eric Sloane.

25. Van Woerkom, Dorothy. My autographed copy from Colvin and Jerry Ann Reid. *Tall Corn: A Tall Tale,* by Dorothy O. Van Woerkom, illustrated by Joe Boddy. St. Louis, Missouri: Milliken 1987. "The Reading Well Series." ISBN# 0-88335-730-5. The

series editors were Patricia and Fred McKis-sack, popular children's authors.

26. *Signing Made Easy* by Rod R. But-terworth and Mickey Flodin. A Perigee Book. New York: Putnam Publishing Group, 1989, p. 61.

27. *Ibid.*, p. 105.

28. My school principal, Alton Du-Rocher, so liked the idea he asked me to bud-get a second rocking chair!

29. Written by the author when teach-ing young children. For Destiny Gullion, who asked questions and for Amber, Tessie, and Traci.

30. Much learning is direct but I learned this song in quite an indirect way. Autumn was beautiful in the Smoky Moun-tains when in 1975 I attended a Children's Curriculum Writer's Conference in Ashe-ville, North Carolina. En route to the air-port, Johnny, the driver, taught me "The Flea Scale" which he had learned from Linda Boyd in Missouri!

31. Hebrew scripture records the wis-dom regarding time and the world in the words of King Solomon. The famous "Time for Everything" passage is Ecclesiastes 3: 1–8. Quoted here are excerpts from the *New Inter-national Version of the Bible*, verses 1a, 4b, and 7b.

32. Finger play from Miss Frances Eliz-abeth Ward, kindergarten education teacher, Mississippi State College for Women, Columbus, Mississippi (now M.U.W).

33. Finger play from Sharon Kerlec, developmental kindergarten teacher when I was school librarian at Allemands Elemen-tary in Des Allemands, Louisiana.

34. Finger play from Roseanne Jarrell, second grade teacher, Allemands.

35. *Ring a Ring o'* Roses, p. 68. My own children heard New Orleans channel 4 tele-vision's "Miss Linda" sing the theme song of "Romper Room School."

36. *Ibid.*, p. 37.

37. *Ibid.*, p. 39.

38. Two versions are given of "The Wiggles." This version, one of my staple finger plays, is from Miss Ward, MSCW, *op. cit.*

39. *Ring a Ring o' Roses, op. cit.*, p. 39.

40. *Ibid.*, p. 40.

41. *Ibid.*, p. 37.

42. *Ibid.*, p. 37.

43. *Ibid.*, p. 40.

44. *Ibid.*, p. 41.

Chapter 4: Rhythm of the ABC's, Signs and Signals

45. My autographed copy came from ALA in Dallas where I met the Hagues.

46. Harris, Karen. My friend Karen Harris, graduate school professor, was enthusiastic about this book, thus so was I. My family gave me a birthday copy.

47. Morris, James Polk III, Ph.D. Thanks for this helpful insight years ago.

48. *Books for the Gifted Child*, Barbara Holland Baskin and Karen Holland Harris. New York: R. R. Bowker, 1980, p. 84. Per-missions letter to Bowker in Reed-Elsevier Group.

49. Baskin and Harris, *Books for the Gifted Child, op. cit.*, p. 184. Though the authors in this quote were specifically refer-ring to *Cathedral: The Story of Its Construc-tion* (1973), the words could refer to many of Macaulay's books.

50. Macaulay, David. Get these books from your library: *Cathedral* (1973); *City* (1974); *Pyramid* (1975); *Underground* (1976); *Castle* (1977); *Unbuilding* (1980); *Mill* (1983). As a child David loved to construct things: elevators from cigar boxes, cable cars from yarn. Later he drew and earned a degree in architecture. His books are for children and also used in college architec-ture classes.

51. *Eight Hands Round: A Patchwork Alphabet*. By Ann Whitford Paul. Illustrated by Jeanette Winter. HarperCollins, 1991. ISBN: 0-06-024704-5.

52. Rather than ten, I would like for the illustrator to have shown eight hands or even

eight people around the quilt on the book cover.

53. Maneval, Max and Betty. Experienced square-dancers, Betty and Max confirmed these directions.

54. Statistic verified by Ivey P. Wallace, Supervisor at Gallaudet, telephone interview, March 17, 1999.

55. *Signing Made Easy* by Rod R. Butterworth and Mickey Flodin. A Perigee Book, The Penguin Putnam Inc. Publishing Group, 1989, p. 13. Thanks to Florence B. Eichin, permissions manager.

56. Butterworth and Flodin, *op. cit.,* p. 219.

57. Thanks to Shelley Trahan for this clever observation.

Chapter 5: Rhythm and Rhyme in Singing

58. *Ring a Ring o' Roses, op. cit.*, p. 34.

59. Music was important in the rural public school and community of my childhood. Both Miss Sue Wheeler at church and Mrs. Daisy Key in school had us dancing like red, yellow, and brown autumn leaves. I only knew the first verse until the 1960s when I began teaching in Natchez. First and second graders enjoy showing motions for verses 2 and 3.

60. Spier, Peter. This large book is excellent for using the colorful double-page spreads to show in a storytime. Obtain the out-of-print title (Doubleday, 1988) from your school or public library.

61. Annually the International Reading Association and the Children's Book Council Joint Committee sponsors the "Children's Choices" project. Five regions of the United States are selected. Nationwide librarians and classroom teachers cooperate in reading books to children and letting them vote on their favorites. As a graduate school student my teacher, Karen Harris, was chosen as a team leader and the University of New Orleans and the New Orleans area selected as a site. The list of books selected is the

choices of children not adults. Write for the annual list published by the IRA. Or write for an annotated version of the list with complete bibliographic information in each October issue of *The Reading Teacher*. See addresses in Appendix B, p. 161.

62. Rhea, *op. cit.*, Two songs reproduced on p. 71.

63. Children like the repetition and rhythm of the Indian chant "Grinding Corn." Use in November or any appropriate time. You can "play this on the piano" by following the directions on p. 77.

64. To make a useful "tape curl" simply tear off a piece of cellophane or masking tape and connect the two ends together, sticky side out. Useful to hang-up paper without showing tape.

Chapter 6: The Rhythm of Music

65. Found in an attic in my hometown, this book belonged to the teacher for whom my elementary school was named. Maude Arnette retired before I started first grade. The songbook was a gift when I began working on this book.

66. *The Rural School Song Book*. Prepared by M. Schoen and Sidney G. Gilbreath. New York: A. S. Barnes, 1919, page iii.

67. "Good Morning to You," 1893.

68. *Songs We Sing from Rodgers and Hammerstein*, Simon and Schuster, 1957. From my St. Charles Parish Library, Norco branch in the Juvenile Collection.

69. *Ibid.*, from *South Pacific*.

70. *Ibid.*

71. *Ibid.*, from *The King and I*.

72. *Ibid.*

73. Music is a great communicator. Bill and I visited China with the American Southern Chorale, Dr. D. Royce Boyer, director; Jan M. Evers, assistant; Nancy C. Edmonson, pianist. We sang to enthusiastic audiences in Beijing, Suzhou, Hangzhou, and Shanghai. These friendly ladies delighted us with their song and dance.

74. *Songs We Sing..., op. cit.*

75. *Ibid.*, from *Oklahoma!*

76. *Ibid.*

77. *Ibid.*, from *Carousel.*

78. *Ibid.*

79. *Ibid.*

80. *Ibid.*

81. *Milton Cross' Encyclopedia of the Great Composers and Their Music*, by Milton Cross and David Ewen. Two Volumes. Doubleday, 1953, 1962. Permission granted by Doubleday (a division of Random House, Inc.). Reference for this quote re Bach from vol. I, pp. 15, 17, 21.

82. *Ibid.*, Beethoven, vol. I, p. 47.

83. Ashton-Warner, Sylvia. *Teacher.* Simon and Schuster, 1963, pp. 15–16.

84. Cross, Milton, *op. cit.*, Brahms, vol. I, p. 118.

85. *Ibid.*, vol. I, Debussy, p. 204.

86. *Ibid.*, vol. I, Elgar, p. 250.

87. *Ibid.*, vol. I, Elgar p. 244.

88. *Ibid.*, vol. I, Gershwin, p. 291.

89. *World Book Encyclopedia*, vol. 8, "G," p. 388.

90. Cross, Milton, *op. cit*, vol. I, Haydn, p. 365.

91. *Ibid.*, vol. II, Mozart, pp. 513–514.

92. *Ibid.*, Mozart, p. 524.

93. *Ibid.*, Prokofiev, p. 577.

94. *Ibid.*, Cross called Prokofiev's *Peter and the Wolf* a symphonic fairy tale, p. 578.

95. *Ibid.*, Prokofiev, p. 583.

96. *Ibid.*, p. 575.

97. *Ibid.*

98. *Ibid.*, Ravel, p. 611.

99. *Ibid.*, p. 615.

100. *Ibid.*, p. 613.

101. *Ibid.*, p. 619.

102. *Ibid.*, p. 614.

103. *Ibid.*, Rimsky-Korsakov, p. 629.

104. *Ibid.*

105. *Ibid.*, p. 636.

106. *Ibid.*, Saint-Saens, p. 657.

107. *Ibid.* Italics mine. Teacher, you too will influence children. "His teacher became such a source of inspiration that Tchaikovsky overcame his natural tendency toward indolence and worked hard and well," p. 795.

108. *Ibid.*, p. 810.

109. *Ibid.*, p. 810.

Chapter 7: Rhythms, Poems, and Poets

110. When Hillery returned home from Niece, France, I wrote and thanked her for the nice note from my niece in Niece. Play with the sound and rhythm of words in your classroom. Read this rhyme about "Rain" anytime and enjoy the rhythm.

111. Halloran, Phyllis. I learned the rhyme "Rain" from Phyllis at Loyola University in New Orleans in a Learning Institute Course: "Reading: Reaching Every Child K–8," Fall 1983.

112. "The Bear Hunt" and "Teddy Bear" are in *Ring a Ring o' Roses, op. cit.* "The Bear Hunt" has also been done in a lovely small edition. Retold by Michael Rosen and illustrated by Helen Oxenbury, *We're Going on a Bear Hunt* (Simon and Schuster, 1989). Small edition, 1992.

113. Caughman, Ginger. "Breakfast." First printed in youth periodical *Event*, July 1982, vol. 12, no. 10, p. 22. Lifeway, used by permission.

114. Bagert, Brod. *Chicken Socks* (Wordsong, 1993) is my favorite of Bagert's books. The poet travels about the country speaking to children, librarians, and teachers, reading aloud his rhymes. He believes poetry should be read aloud.

115. Arbuthnot, May Hill, *op. cit.*, p. 161.

116. *Ibid.*, p. 168.

117. Bartlett's, *op. cit.*, p. 668.

118. Bagert, Brod. *op. cit.* Thanks again to "the three chickens" who gave this book to me: Lori, Sharon and Debbie on February 25, 1994.

119. Greenfield, Eloise. Eloise Greenfield received support from the Commission on the Arts and Humanities and the National Endowment for the Arts in Washington, D.C., for this poetry collection.

120. Koch, Kenneth. *Rose, Where Did*

You Get That Red? Teaching Great Poetry to Children. Vintage (Random House), 1973, pp. 3–4.

121. *Ibid.*, p. 4.
122. *Ibid.*, p. 35.
123. *Ibid.*, p. 287.
124. *Ibid.*, p. 308.
125. Cummings, Margaret Ann. These haiku (Japanese nature poems) were printed in a children's paper, *Adventure*, November 16, 1975. "Haiku for You." Nashville: Broadman. Used by permission.
126. Thanks to my friend, Margaret N. Powe, for this idea. She practices this system in her busy job as director, Council on Aging, St. Charles Parish. Have a special place for a project meaningful to you. Give the project priority.
127. Delaneuville, Laura. Thank you Laura, for permission to quote from your poem and for the artwork by Alexis.

Chapter 8: Rhythm of Color and Art

128. Color Dots. A student once gave me a bookmark covered with tiny colorful dots made with felt-tip markers. When I asked: "Did you know there was an artist who painted with little dots?" he was fascinated. We looked up the name Georges Seurat (French artist, 1859–1891) in the library. Librarians regularly teach one on one by helping students focus their interests and attention through research.
129. Do not buy a cheap brand of crayons. I simply like "Crayola" the best. The brand name is used by permission.
130. Thanks to Coral Molchanoff and Natalie O'Regan.
131. Thank you dear Katelyn Rose, Sharon Rose, and Nell Rose.
132. Many thanks to Mary and Jacob Marino for kitchen testing and to Pam Troxler for the name.
133. Red in French is "rouge." The film *Le Ballon Rouge* and the paperback book *The Red Balloon* are copyrighted by Albert Lamorisse, 1956
134. The zester is fun to use. My zester, made in Germany, came from Calgary, Canada.

Chapter 9: Rhythm of Play

135. "Fun Play, Safe Play: A Guide from the American Toy Institute, Inc." New revised toy safety brochure. Quotes in Chapter 9 regarding toys and play are from this brochure and used with permission. Thanks to Andrew Au, communications assistant. To order copies of this booklet see address and website in Appendix B, p. 159.
136. *Ibid.*, p. 7.
137. *Ibid.*, p. 8.
138. *Ibid.*, p. 9.
139. *Ibid.*, p. 10.
140. *Ibid.*, p. 11.
141. *Webster's Dictionary.*
142. American Toy Institute, p. 11.
143. *Ibid.*, p. 12.
144. Hoban, Tana. Hoban has won prizes as a photographer and filmmaker and has exhibited at the Museum for Modern Art in NYC. Look for her many concept books in your library. Of her own work she says: "My books are about noticing things."
145. American Toy Institute, p. 13.

Chapter 10: Rhythm of Seasons

146. Smells evoke many memories. Thanks to this delicious hint and other pumpkin tips from Joyce Deaner who sells pumpkins and mums. "Carving Pumpkin Perfectly," article by Rosalyn Dunn, *The Times-Picayune*, October 27, 1998, p. F5.
147. Obtain free or inexpensive newsprint end rolls from a newspaper or printing office.
148. Cross, Milton. *op. cit.*, vol. 2, Tchaikovsky, p. 810.
149. Thanks to Marsha Jenkins, sister of Michelle Carmouche, for the clever idea and for my stick-horse Christmas ornament.

150. Pushker, Gloria. Gloria Teles Pushker, who teachers children's literature at Loyola University in New Orleans, has written some books about Toby Belfer, a Jewish girl in South Louisiana. The one appropriate for young children in the focus of this book is *Toby Belfer Never Had a Christmas Tree* (Pelican, 1991). This picture book explains Hanukkah in an informative story.

151. Teachers, adapt your oral directions as needed if you have students who are left-handed. Thanks Stacy Mohundro, for teaching me the needs of "lefties."

152. Paper tearing can be used in many ways. Make quick name tags. Tear only a simple outline or shape. Do not try to include details. I first learned of this technique from Elsie Rives at a children's conference at Glorieta, New Mexico. Elsie was co-author of the now out-of-print title *Guiding Children*, Elsie Rives and Margaret Sharpe, Nashville: Convention, 1969, p. 36. I later taught this book in Louisiana conferences.

153. Used with permission of the Cornell Lab of Ornithology in Ithaca, New York. Thanks to Margaret A. Barker.

154. Cornell's "Project Feeder Watch" is for classrooms, schools, home-schools, or groups, such as Scouts or 4-H. "Participants watch birds every two weeks from November through March. You count the kinds and numbers of birds at your feeders and send the data to Cornell Lab for analysis. Your class can spend as little or as much time as you want." For more information write or call Cornell Lab of Ornithology. See Cornell in Appendix B for address, p. 159.

155. Cohen's boon, Greenwillow (Morrow), 1979.

Appendix A: Snacks and Recipes

156. "Thank you, Sam-I-Am!" to Sharon Kerlec and class who served this school librarian green eggs as a surprise after a week of reading *Green Eggs and Ham* to all the developmental-kindergarten through grade two classes at Allemands, October 1987.

Appendix B: Resources and Addresses

157. Letter from Ellyn Scott, consumer affairs manager, Binney and Smith, Inc. July 29, 1996.

158. Telephone conversation and email, Debi Lindaberry, Binney and Smith Consumer Center, April 15, 1999.

159. The word "Crayola" in this book is used with permission of Binney and Smith, Inc., with special thanks to Debi Lindaberry, licensing and trademark administrator, April 20, 1999. See p. 159.

160. Sloane, Eric. *op. cit.*

Index